NEWSPAPER ETHICS IN
THE NEW CENTURY

Newspaper Ethics in the New Century

*A Report to the
American Society of
Newspaper Editors*

EDITED BY

Philip Meyer

AMERICAN SOCIETY OF NEWSPAPER EDITORS

Reston, Virginia

ISBN 1-59460-255-7
LCCN 2006923719

American Society of Newspaper Editors
11690B Sunrise Valley Drive
Reston, VA 20191-1409

Produced and distributed by
Carolina Academic Press
700 Kent Street
Durham, NC 27701
Telephone (919)929-8829
Fax (919) 493-5668
www.cap-press.com

Printed in the United States of America

CONTENTS

Introduction
vii

CHAPTER 1
The New Editor-Publisher Relationship
Rachel Davis Mersey
3

CHAPTER 2
Blogging to Stay in the Black
Robin Roger
13

CHAPTER 3
This Just In: Not All Journalists Are Miserable
Caroline K. Hauser
19

CHAPTER 4
News Gathering: On Shaky Ground?
Erik Holmes
31

CHAPTER 5
Fading Freedom: The Changing Role of Ombudsmen
Jonathan Bloom
41

CHAPTER 6
Newspapers and the Right to Privacy: New Rules?
Casey Ferrell
53

CHAPTER 7
Diversity in Newsrooms: A Path toward Improvement?
Nicole Elise Smith
61

CHAPTER 8
Financial Conflicts of Interest
Rita F. Colistra
71

CHAPTER 9
Non-Financial Conflicts of Interest
Nathan Clendenin
85

CHAPTER 10
None of This Is Made Up: Fabrication and Plagiarism
Gabriel Dance
91

CHAPTER 11
Protecting Sources
Anne J. Tate
97

CHAPTER 12
Declining Support for News Councils
Ryan Campbell
107

A 2005 Survey of Concerns
of Newspaper People
115

Introduction

When ASNE commissioned its 1982 study of newspaper ethics, its main goal was to improve the relationship between editors and their publishers in defining professional values. The close collaboration between Katharine Graham and Ben Bradlee as they handled the Washington Post's Watergate investigation was still fresh in memory. Not all publishers, that survey revealed, were as bold, socially conscious, or as trusting of their editor as Graham.

Today's concerns are more basic. As newspaper readership declines and news-editorial resources are depleted, new kinds of pressures on traditional ethical values are created. There is anecdotal evidence to suggest that publishers are infringing on editors' territory as they strive to maintain traditional profit levels even as circulation declines. But the evidence in these pages by the 12 authors of this report suggests that the anecdotes are not representative. Editor autonomy has improved since the 1982 survey. Editor-publisher relationships are smoother. And there is little indication that the drive for profit has led to a general decline in ethical standards.

These conclusions are the product of my fall 2005 seminar on media analysis in the School of Journalism and Mass Communication at the University of North Carolina at Chapel Hill. Rachel Davis Mersey assisted with the editing of this volume.

The original 1982 survey was funded by the John and Mary R. Markle foundation with field work by the Research Triangle Institute. The 2005 survey was funded by Paul McCreath and the James Franceschini Foundation with field work by FGI of Chapel Hill.

Both surveys used a sample selection procedure based on newspaper circulation. We used ABC data for member papers and the Editor & Publisher Yearbook for non-members to list all daily newspapers in the USA by their circulation. The probability of selection into the sample was in proportion to circulation size. Thus the percentages reported reflect not the percent of editors or staff members who responded but the percent of total daily newspaper circulation that those editors and staffers represent. For example, a response from an editor of a 300,000 circulation paper is given 10 times the weight of one whose paper has 30,000 circulation. This procedure makes the data for 1982 and 2005 comparable and reflects the investigators' concern for the social effects of newspaper's moral values. This selection process yielded 566 newspapers. Another 32 were added for a data sharing project with the Readership Institute at Northwestern University and are not included in this analysis.

The top editors at each paper were identified by the ASNE staff. Newspaper staff members were chosen from the Editor & Publisher Yearbook, the membership list of the American Copy Editors Society, and page-one bylines obtained from the Internet. The identification and selection procedures were different in 1982 but not in a way that would be expected to influence the results. Exact wording of the questions is reproduced in the appendix to this report.

Data were collected using a self-administered questionnaire sent by mail with three follow-ups. The initial mailing to editors and staff members was on July 12, 2005, and the last counted response was received on Sept. 13, 2005. Response rate in the 2005 survey was 71 percent for editors and 64 percent for staff members—high for mail surveys, but not as high as the 1982 responses, which were 78 and 72 percent respectively. We take this as a sign that editors are much busier these days.

Philip Meyer
Chapel Hill
February 2006

NEWSPAPER ETHICS IN THE NEW CENTURY

CHAPTER 1

THE NEW
EDITOR-PUBLISHER
RELATIONSHIP

Rachel Davis Mersey

The editor-publisher relationship has evolved visibly since 1982. Editors in this new century are more assertive and more independent. And some have been bold enough to gain influence on the business side of the paper while becoming less tolerant of publisher pressure on the editorial side. Both editors and their staff members saw their publisher's involvement in the newsroom as more benign in 2005 than they did in 1982.

This trend turned up in the survey despite recent some high-profile anecdotes to the contrary. For example, *Miami Herald* publisher, Jesus Diaz Jr., participated in the firing of columnist Jim DeFede for the undisclosed taping of a phone conversation with former city commissioner Arthur E. Teele Jr. just before Teele's very public suicide. In his brief stint as publisher of the *Los Angeles Times*, Mark H. Willes issued a "vow to reinvent the newspaper business by detonating the wall between editorial and business departments." Despite widespread criticism of his deal with the Staples Center for a promotional supplement, he claimed to have replaced the wall with " 'lines' of authority that 'appropriately demarcate areas of responsibility.' "[1] And, at a 2003 joint conference of the New England Newspaper Association and the New England Society of Newspaper Editors, Dean Singleton, vice chairman and chief executive officer of Denver-based MediaNews Group, Inc., admitted "regretting his ear-

---

1. Carol Guensburg, "A Painful Decision," *American Journalism Review* (July/ Aug. 1999): 88.

lier firing of a *Times of Trenton* reporter for not printing an advertiser's press release verbatim."[2] At the same meeting, *Boston Herald* publisher Patrick Purcell, who had been accused three years earlier "of softening his paper's aggressive coverage of a bank merger," offered this insight: "I don't have a lot of sympathy with editors; lots of papers have gone out of business because of people digging in too deeply. I'd rather see a paper survive and be smart about how we handle certain situations."[3]

Such incidents might be more likely to come to the surface today, but the data suggest that they are not more common. The publisher's dilemma is an old one. In 1986, Purdue University's John Webster said, "Newspaper publishers today are caught in an ethical dilemma, being admonished on one hand to follow the newsroom ideal to observe their community with objective detachment and on the other to assist with community economic and social development even to the point of personal participation in civic promotional projects."[4]

This conflict potentially affects editors, who need a steady advertising revenue stream to support an adequate staff and extend their editorial reach to new means of distribution on the Internet.

"Management and editorial in the modern newsroom may not agree on much, but they seem to agree that the other side needs to be set right on where [the] 'walls' [dividing them] stand and how 'church and state' is to be separated," said Thomas Leonard in a 2000 *Columbia Journalism Review* article. "It is an odd way to think. A wall blocks the vision of people on either side of it. Churches have to raise money."

And so, the reasoning goes, do newspapers.

The 2005 survey replicates several questions from 1982 in an attempt to determine what has changed.

---

2. Bill Kirtz, "Editors and Publishers: A Marriage," *Poynter Online* (Nov. 14, 2003), http://www.poynter.org/content/content_view.asp?id=54506 (accessed Sept. 13, 2005).

3. Ibid.

4. John Webster, "The Publisher and Civic Activity: Civic Activism Dilemma," *Journal of Mass Media Ethics* (Fall/Winter 1986–87): 41.

Defining the Editor's Role

Both the 1982 and 2005 surveys asked about the ideal and actual roles of the editor. Respondents were asked which of this list of possibilities was preferable and then which actually existed at his or her paper.

(1) The editor should participate fully in financial planning and marketing decisions.

(2) The editor should be kept fully informed of financial planning and marketing decisions, but should participate only when questions related to his specific expertise are involved.

(3) The editor should be kept informed of financial planning and marketing decisions on a "need-to-know" basis, i.e., whenever his help is needed in carrying out the decisions.

(4) The editor should be insulated from all financial planning and marketing decisions so that he can concentrate on putting out the paper.

Editors changed little in their perceptions of how they should operate. Those representing 45 percent of circulation wanted full participation in 1982 compared to 41 percent in 2005. But the gap between their desires and the actuality had virtually closed by the time of the second survey. Table 1 shows that by 2005, the gap was a trivial 2 percentage points (41 v. 39).

Table 1 The gap between what editors want and what they get, 1982 and 2005

	1982 desire	1982 actual	2005 desire	2005 actual
(1) **Participate fully**	45%	28%	41%	39%
(2) **Fully informed**	39	33	47	41
(3) **Need-to-know basis**	14	35	11	19
(4) **Insulated**	2	4	1	1
Total	100%	100%	100%	100%

Staff members in both time periods had lower estimates of editors' involvement in financial issues, and they were less approving. The proportion who thought editors should fully participate decreased from 20 percent in 1982 to 10 percent in 2005.

Knowing the new expectations of the editor's role, we can focus now on how the editor relates to the publisher.

Defining the Publisher's Role

We know that in today's business environment in light of dwindling readership, publishers are experiencing pressure from a variety of sources that might be impacting their position and their relationship with the newsroom.

"The relationship between editors and publishers [is] arguably the most important relationship at a newspaper in terms of quality of journalism that ultimately gets done," argued Brent Cunningham in a 2000 *Columbia Journalism Review* article.[5] "The relationship has changed because the news business has changed. It has become more business-like, complete with sophisticated marketing techniques perfected in corporate America."[6]

Jay Harris, former publisher of Knight Ridder's San Jose *Mercury News*, identified business infringement on the newsroom as the reason for his sudden resignation in 2001. "What troubled me most about the meeting [of *Mercury News* and Knight Ridder executives] was its myopic focus on numbers. It wasn't the cutting so much. I have cut and forced others to over many years. I was taught how to do so by the best on both sides of the table. What troubled me — something that had never happened to me before in all my years in the company — was that little or no attention was paid to the consequences of achieving 'the number.' There was virtually no discussion of the damage that would be done to the quality and aspirations of the *Mercury News* as a journalistic endeavor or to its ability to fulfill its responsibilities to the community."[7]

---

5. Brent Cunningham, "Publishers and Editors: The Most Important Relationship," *Columbia Journalism Review* (May/June 2000): 32.

6. Ibid., 33.

7. Jay Harris in a speech to the American Society of Newspaper Editors,

But how has this new environment impacted the publisher? In considering this evolving role, scholar John Webster recognized, "A publisher's leadership model utilized in addressing community, business, and constituent loyalties is birthed in the process of invention, in the construction of a decision-making plan created from his/her broadest and most adventurous vision."[8]

How is that vision being implemented in newsrooms today? Both the 1982 and 2005 ASNE surveys asked several questions aimed at understanding the general role of the publisher and pinpointing the presence of specific unwanted behaviors.

First, respondents were asked,

> Newspapers vary greatly in the amount of involvement that publishers have in the news operations. Here are four statements describing different levels of publisher involvement. Regardless of how things work at your paper, which of the following statements comes closest to describing the way you think *publishers* ought to operate:
>
> (1) The publisher should always be involved in deciding what appears in his or her newspaper on a day-to-day basis.
>
> (2) The publisher should generally be involved in deciding what appears in his or her newspaper over the long run, but not on a daily basis.
>
> (3) The publisher should be involved in hiring good people to run the news operation, but not in deciding what appears in the paper. The publisher's only intervention in the news operation should be to hire or fire the editor.
>
> (4) The publisher should have nothing whatsoever to do with the news operation.

Among editors the most noticeable shift across time is occurring in the middle categories (see table 2).

---

http://www.poynter.org/content/content_view.asp?id=4109 (accessed Sept. 13, 2005).

8. John Webster, "The Publisher and Civic Activity: Civic Activism Dilemma," *Journal of Mass Media Ethics* (Fall/Winter 1986–87): 45.

Table 2 Editors' opinions of how publishers ought to operate, 1982 and 2005

	1982	2005
(1) **Always involved**	2%	2%
(2) **Generally involved**	58	48
(3) **Hiring and firing only**	36	48
(4) **Not involved**	5	2
Total	100%[a]	100%

[a] Percent adds to more than 100 because of rounding.

In 1982, editors representing almost 60 percent of circulation favored their publisher being generally involved in the newsroom. The down-the-middle split in 2005 marks a shift in editors' preferences toward lessened publisher participation in the newsroom.

The movement across time among staff members tilts in the same direction (see table 3).

Table 3 Staff members' opinions of how publishers ought to operate, 1982 and 2005

	1982	2005
(1) **Always involved**	1%	4%
(2) **Generally involved**	54	29
(3) **Hiring and firing only**	43	59
(4) **Not involved**	2	8
Total	100%	100%

In 1982, staff members representing 55 percent of newspaper readers believed their publisher should be always or generally involved in the news side. In the 2005 data, only about a third felt that way. Like editors, staff member preferences leaned more toward a remote publisher in the second survey.

Did the publisher's actual behavior follow these changing expectations? The survey asked this question,

> Now you have told us how publishers *should* operate, please indicate which of the four comes closest to the way things actually work at your paper.

With this, editors confirmed a behavioral shift among their publishers across time (see table 4). From 1982 to 2005, there was a 10-percentage point drop in editors who see their publisher as always or generally involved in the editorial workings of their newspaper. Staff members tended to see the same trend.

Table 4 Editors' opinions of how publishers actually operate, 1982 and 2005

	1982	2005
(1) **Always involved**	3%	4%
(2) **Generally involved**	61	50
(3) **Hiring and firing only**	32	42
(4) **Not involved**	4	4
Total	100%	100%

Bad Publishers

What are the dangers of close publisher involvement in the newsroom? The 1982 survey measured the frequency of four specific behaviors to form an index of "malign publisher participation."[9] Explained Meyer: "The substance of what we are looking for is too important to risk on a single question in a survey. There is too much room for error in the response to one question. What the questioner had in mind and what the respondent thinks is being asked about may be quite different. The safe thing to do is to compile a number of questions that measure pretty much the same thing, ask them all, and then combine them into an index."[10]

These are the indicators of the malign index:

(1) How often does the publisher of your paper ask for special handling of an article about a company or organization which has some economic clout over your newspaper?
(2) How often does the publisher ask for special handling of an article about an organization or individual with whom he has strong social ties?

---

9. Meyer, *Ethical Journalism*, 100–102.
10. Ibid., 100.

(3) How often does the publisher ask the editor to send a reporter on a non-news mission for the company: to influence legislation, for example, or gather information on the competition?

(4) How often, to the best of your knowledge, does your paper publish editorial matter controlled by the business office on behalf of advertisers in the news columns (commonly known as "blurbs" or "business office musts")?

Factor analysis, the method employed to determine if questions are all examining the same underlying concept, confirmed that these four indicators still hold together as a measure of malign publisher behavior. To aggregate them, we assign publishers a score from 0, for one who never engages in any of the specified behaviors, to 4, for one who employs all of them even if infrequently. A comparison over time is then possible. Table 5 reports editors' perceptions.

Table 5 Index of Malign Publisher Participation, 1982 and 2005[a]

	1982 frequency	2005 frequency
0	30%	42%
1	22	24
2	23	20
3	18	13
4	7	2

[a] Percents may add to more than 100 because of rounding.

According to this index, editors' perceptions of their publisher's negative involvement in the newsroom have dissipated markedly. In 2005, editors representing more than 40 percent of newspaper circulation indicated that their publishers participated in none of the four malign behaviors, a 12 percentage-point jump in 23 years—a positive sign that publishers are behaving.

Another way to look at the same information is that proportion of publishers committing two or more of the listed infractions decreased from nearly half in 1982 to about a third in 2005.

Comparing Publisher Types

Does publisher behavior matter? Consider the relationship between a publisher's rank on the malign index, from 0 to 4, and editors' perception of morale. Editors were asked to rate the morale in their newsroom during the past few months on a scale of 1 to 10, with 10 being the happiest possible newsroom and 1 being the least happy.

Newsrooms with the best behaved publishers, those with a zero on the malign scale, were happier than the others—by 6.85 to 6.63 as estimated by editors on the 10-point morale scale. That might not sound like much, but it is statistically significant, given the way responses were tightly packed around the center of the scale.

Morale estimates by staff members revealed the same effect, but it was small and not distinguishable from sampling error.

The malign publisher index suggests another question. What kinds of organizations produce these publishers? Are privately or publicly held companies more likely to host publishers high on the malign index? A simple crosstab allows us to see this (Table 6).

Table 6 Ownership status and Malign Publisher Index, 2005[a]

	Private	Public
0	27%	55%
1	28	21
2	26	14
3	16	9
4	3	1

[a] Editors only

By a margin of 28 percentage points, the readers served by the best kind of publishers, those that practice a healthy editorial and business separation, are most likely to be reading investor-owned newspapers.

Conclusion

The 2005 ASNE survey generally holds good news for the newspaper business. Today, publishers are less likely to be involved in the manipulation of editorial influence, and editors are more likely to be fully informed of financial planning and marketing decisions. The wall that once segregated editorial and business may have been traded for a strong bridge.

While staff members are more likely than editors to favor a separation of their newspaper's editorial and business sides, a trend that has proven true over time, editors tend to favor participation in financial planning and marketing decisions. And they are doing it.

Simultaneously, the data indicate that editors and staff members favor lessened publisher participation in the newsroom. Despite their concerns, editors' perceptions of their publisher's negative involvement in the newsroom have dissipated drastically. Publishers are doing less interfering and making more ethical decisions—in the eyes of editors today—than they were in 1982.

Further attention to publisher behavior suggests a high level of influence on additional variables. According to editors and staff members, the best publishers are likely to have the happiest newsrooms. Publisher involvement is okay if it is does done for good purposes.

The fact that publishers have this opportunity may be exactly what the news business needs right now. In his farewell speech to ASNE, Jay Harris said, "It is good that we have people working for reform inside and outside the newspaper business. When Martin Luther nailed his Ninety-five Theses on the door of the church in Wittenberg, near the beginning of what we now call the Reformation, there were people of good will working at nearly every level of the Catholic Church. Those, like Luther, who left the church to protest its debasement, and the many who remained to work for improvement from within, gave rise not only to a new branch of Christianity, the Protestants, but also forced the reform of the Catholic Church. Much of the same needs to happen today. A publisher wrote me this week to say he respected my decision to resign and hoped I would respect his decision to stay in the job and put out the best paper he could for his community. And that newspaper is still quite good. Not only do I respect his decision, I know it is the right one if we are to set the balance right again. We need people like that publisher working on the inside to support good journalism and build healthy businesses."

CHAPTER 2

Blogging to Stay in the Black

Robin Roger

As technology advances and young readers increasingly turn to the Internet for news, editors are searching for ways to revive their newspapers. Weblogs, or blogs, have become the latest hope in the quest for the young audience. Early adopters include the *Chicago Tribune*, *The Sacramento Bee*, and the *Greensboro* (N.C.) *News & Record*. Different newspapers use their blogs differently, but most of them aim to increase readership or maintain existing readership, while contributing to the democratic aims of the mass media—to inform the public. As the previous chapter revealed, more editors have become involved in the financial decisions at their newspapers, allowing them to have greater influence in deciding the future of the newspaper.

Declining circulation of print newspapers has made the industry more willing to experiment.[1] Blogging is one manifestation. Radical experiments such as these hold the potential to reshape the business, and the creation of blogs could redefine the boundary between the business side and the editorial side of news organizations, a concern that is examined from different angles in Chapter 1 (editor—publisher relationships), Chapter 8 (financial conflict of interests) and Chapter 9 (non-financial conflict of interests). Traditionally, these two spheres have experienced a separation likened to church and state. And although advertiser influence on content is usually frowned upon, experimenting with content based on market research is nothing new.

The proliferation of technology creates both dangers and opportunities. It seems logical that editors who have a foot in the business

---

1. The Audit Bureau of Circulation's September 2005 audit of 789 newspapers recorded a 2.6 percent decline in daily paid circulation in the previous year.

world would be more likely to push for technological innovation to save their trade.

Blogs have opened up the discourse with the news audience, creating a many-to-many conversation, rather than a one-to-many lecture.[2] As a mass medium, newspapers traditionally carry out a one-to-many discourse, with the exception of letters to the editor. Of course, not all of the letters submitted are published and some newspapers have a limit on how often each letter writer can get published. The more democratic nature of blogs can open up a public forum and give readers greater opportunities to voice their opinions.

Newspaper blogs also allow for transparency. Reporters can outline their writing process, explaining their newsgathering techniques and how they decided what to include and what to leave out. Editors can explain the stories they pick for the front page and the tough daily choices they make, such as whether or not to run a sensitive photo. This transparency can create trust, something newspapers are losing with their readers. In contrast, Thomas Johnson and Barbara Kaye found that Weblog users rated them as more credible than traditional media sources, including newspapers and broadcast news.[3]

While transparency and dialog have become crucial for businesses in the wired age, it is not clear how newspapers can make money from blogs.[4] While many blogs contain ads, it will take much experimentation to find out how to present them and charge for them.

---

2. Brian Carroll, "Culture Clash: Journalism and the Communal Ethos of the Blogosphere," in *Into the Blogosphere: Rhetoric, Community, and Culture of Weblogs*, ed. Laura Gurak, Smiljana Antonijevic, Laurie Johnson, Clancy Ratliff, and Jessica Reyman, http://blog.lib.umn.edu/blogosphere/culture_clash_journalism_and_the_communal_ethos_of_the_blogosphere.html (accessed Aug. 13, 2004).

3. Thomas Johnson and Barbara Kaye, "Wag the Blog: How Reliance on Traditional Media and the Internet Influence Credibility Perceptions of Weblogs among Blog Users," *Journalism & Mass Communication Quarterly* (Autumn 2004): 622–642.

4. Rick Levine, Christopher Locke, Doc Searls, and David Weinberger, *The Cluetrain Manifesto: The End of Business as Usual* (Cambridge, Mass.: Perseus Books Group, 2000).

Some bloggers, such as Jim Romenesko and Matt Drudge have made enough money blogging to make it a full-time job. It remains to be seen, however, if newspapers can make money with blogs. But blogging is a low-cost experiment. When placed alongside glossy specialty publications targeted at young readers, blogs, because of their low distribution cost, might yield a much greater return on investment.

The 2005 ASNE study shows a direct relationship between an editor's involvement in financial matters and a newspaper's likelihood of having a blog. Newspapers with editors who participate fully or are at least fully informed on financial planning and marketing decisions are the most likely to have blogs (see table 1). Among newspapers whose editors are insulated from the business side, a majority, representing 80 percent of that category's daily circulation, have no blog and no plan to start one.

Table 1 Level of editor participation in business decisions and presence of blogs, 2005[a]

	Participate fully	Fully informed	Need-to-know	Insulated
Blog	39%	41%	27%	0%
No blog but considering	46	27	34	20
No blog & no plan to blog	15	32	38	80
Total	100%[b]	100%[b]	100%	100%

[a] Based on responses from editors only
[b] Percent does not add to 100 because of rounding.

Many writers in the trade journals refer to blogging as a survival strategy. The tagline to one article makes the money connection perfectly clear: "With Weblogs all the rage, newspapers try to cash in on the trend. Some sites are even getting overhauls to make them more blogger-friendly."[5] In his August 2005 article in *Quill* magazine, Fred Brown quoted Jeff Jarvis of BuzzMachine, who wrote that new media put traditional journalism in a shadow of defeatism and defiance,

---

5. Jesse Oxfeld, "Blogs Rolling in 2005," *Editor & Publisher* (Jan. 2005): 36–40.

caused by newspapers' inability to make money.[6] Brown wrote "this defeatist mood apparently has led to a certain desperation, recently illustrated by the attempt to make the *Los Angeles Times* editorial page more fun and energetic by making it interactive, employing the Wikipedia model." Brown noted that this attempt failed, but suggested they may have been on to something.[7]

In "Letting the Blogs Out," Jesse Oxfeld wrote about *Greensboro News & Record* Editor John Robinson as a radical. Robinson objects to being called a "radical," Oxfeld said, "but to those who spend time thinking about how, even if newspapers will survive in a super-connected, empowered, non-intermediated, and — here's the word — blogified world, John Robinson is on the barricades."[8] According to Robinson, the *News & Record* started blogging in order to engage readers and to create a town-square atmosphere. Oxfeld concludes, however, that this decision was in some part economic, when he wrote the town-square atmosphere was one "that welcomed, involved, and addressed the concerns of readers — who would then, presumably, continue buying the paper."[9]

Robinson has said, "Any editor who is not involved in financial decisions is an idiot."[10] Being involved, he said, allows him to have input into how the newspaper is marketed and represented to the public. His own blog, http://blog.news-record.com/jrblog/, serves somewhat of a customer service function. He said people outside the newsroom used to write about decisions the paper made and they'd usually assign the worst motives, without asking. Now with his blog, he said, "If they ask, we'll tell them." Of course, the bottom line is not Robinson's only motivation for blogging. He said the blogs are an attempt to build community in a way that a newspaper has never been able to

---

6. Fred Brown, " 'Citizen' Journalism Is Not Professional Journalism," *Quill* 93, no. 6 (Aug. 2005): 42.

7. The attempt failed because users started posting pornographic images. The site subsequently was shut down.

8. Jesse Oxfeld, "Letting the Blogs Out," *Editor & Publisher* (Mar. 2005): 38–42.

9. Ibid., 51.

10. John Robinson, guest speaker in journalism class, University of North Carolina at Chapel Hill, Nov. 10, 2005.

before. He said the greatest aim of the blogs is not to make money—
he has no idea how to do that—but he did say that newspapers have
to figure out a way to do it.

The newspaper business is indeed a business; and those in charge
are doing whatever they can to keep it afloat. Newspapers have
launched a number of experiments, from free-distribution youth
publications to blogs, to gain readership among young people as their
most reliable readers grow older. While some journalists might re
flexively think of making money as a bad thing, others recognize that,
without the money to keep the presses rolling, newspapers will no
longer be able to carry out their democratic mission.

It is the latter viewpoint that is associated with support for blogging. It could also mean that bolder editors feel more empowered to
innovate generally, including experiments with blogs. Causation cannot be proven, and it cannot be determined which happened first.
Did editors become involved in financial matters to counter threats
from technology? Or did they get into the blogging game because of
their appreciation of technology and a desire to engage in the marketing strategies at the newspaper? Either way, technology and the
newspaper business are intertwined, and the editorial side cannot
help but be affected.

CHAPTER 3

THIS JUST IN:
NOT ALL JOURNALISTS ARE MISERABLE

Caroline K. Hauser

There are plenty of tales of woe in the newspaper industry these days, and each one seems to include that stock line: Morale is at an all-time low.

It's not.

Morale among newspaper journalists is up. Since 1982, assessments of newsroom morale by both editors and staff have grown more optimistic. Editors are still prone to overestimate newsroom morale, but they have become slightly more realistic in their estimations.

The 2005 ASNE survey pinpoints the evolution of newsroom culture since 1982. The increase in newsroom morale was only one of the surprises. Another is how editors at newspapers with layoffs and reductions in force fail to see the dramatic and negative influence that makes their newsrooms stark exceptions to the general trend of improved staff morale.

Job satisfaction among journalists is well researched and well documented. David Weaver and G. Cleveland Wilhoit, with a variety of collaborators, have followed trends concerning the American journalist for more than twenty years. Their work makes up the bulk of the American Journalist survey, a decennial measure begun in 1971 by John Johnstone. From 1971 to 1982, and again from 1982 to 1992, Wilhoit and Weaver documented a precipitous decline in newsroom morale. In 1992, the stresses cited most by unhappy journalists were management policies, low salaries and a lack of advancement opportunities. In their 2002 survey, however, Weaver and Wilhoit saw an uptick. After the percentage of journalists who said they were "very satisfied" in their jobs dropped from 49 percent in 1971 to 27 percent in 1992, the six-point bounce in 2002 to 33 percent was welcome news. This long-ranging study is complemented by Johnstone, Wilhoit and Weaver's research investigating the effect of structural and demographic factors on job satisfaction, including salary, supervisors, autonomy, advancement prospects and workplace pride.[1]

However, the increase in morale found in the academic literature finds no counterpart in the trade press. Trade journals such as *Columbia Journalism Review*, *American Journalism Review* and *Quill* turn to that favorite phrase—"Morale was at an all-time low"—when describing cases of layoffs or ethical scandals, and there are plenty of occasions to report on both phenomena. According to the Newspaper Association of America, "Newsrooms lost nearly 1,000 reporters, 600 editors, 300 photographers and artists and just over 400 copy editors, as top editors and publishers in large and small papers reduced staffs to weather the faltering economy" from 2001 to 2005.[2] The October 2004 slashing at the *Dallas Morning News*, in which 65 newsroom employees, slightly more than 10 percent of the paper's journalists, were laid off, is a good example. Charles Layton reported for *AJR*, "The cuts included people with 20 and 30 years' service, people held in extremely high regard by their colleagues, people who had recently won prizes and gotten pay raises and glowing performance reviews from their bosses, and then were suddenly sacked."[3]

Along with layoffs, troubled relationships among publishers, editors and newsrooms are often cited as a drain on morale. In 1998, for example, *AJR* reported on the changes taking place at the *Free Lance-Star* in Fredericksburg, Va.[4] Lori Robertson described "an idyllic newspaper of sorts—a family-owned, high-quality, award-winning,

---

1. For more on the American Journalist survey including methodological details and results, see, "The Face and Mind of the American Journalist: 4th Decennial Survey Finds an Older, Better Paid, More Professional Workforce," *Poynter Online* (Apr. 10, 2003), http://www.poynter.org/content/content_view.asp?id=28235 (accessed Dec. 24, 2005).

2. "Newsroom Staff: 2001-2005," http://www.naa.org/thesource/25.asp (accessed Dec. 24, 2005).

3. Charles Layton, "The Dallas Mourning News," *American Journalism Review* (April/ May 2005), http://www.ajr.org/Article.asp?id=3836 (accessed Dec. 24, 2005).

4. Lori Robertson, "Stormy Weather in Fredericksburg," *American Journalism Review* (Sept. 1998), http://www.ajr.org/Article.asp?id=3444 (accessed Dec. 24, 2005).

highly profitable daily where morale was high and turnover rare"
shook to its core when a new publisher moved the editorial page's ide-
ological center, implemented a redesign, added a Sunday edition,
fired several staffers and caused enough disruption to make several
others quit.[5]

Some newspapers have taken the problem into their own hands.
The *St. Petersburg Times*, for instance, hired a human resources consulting firm in 2004 to survey staff attitudes. The survey asked employees to what extent they agreed or disagreed with statements
such as,

(1) My job provides me with a sense of personal accomplishment;
(2) In response to staffer input, the *St. Petersburg Times* makes real
    changes in the way work is done;
(3) I have the resources necessary to do my job;
(4) I am personally motivated to help the *St. Petersburg Times* be
    successful; and
(5) I would recommend the *St. Petersburg Times* to a friend as a
    good place to work.

In response to the results, the *St. Petersburg Times* began holding
more frequent staff meetings, recommitted to producing timely performance evaluations, offered more training opportunities for more
staffers and formed committees to do the first revision of job descriptions in 12 years, making changes where appropriate. According
to Bill Stevens, an editor at the *St. Petersburg Times*, these changes—
particularly the salary adjustments—boosted morale a good deal.

Morale in Newsrooms Then and Now

Perception of a newsroom's morale depends heavily on perspective.
The 2005 ASNE survey asked editors and newspaper staff members,

How would you rate the morale in your newsroom during the past few months? On a scale of 1 to 10, with 10 being

---

5. Ibid.

the happiest possible newsroom and 1 being the least happy, where would you put yours?

In every measurement taken for this chapter, editors' view of newsroom morale was higher than that of staffers. The mean morale score reported by editors was 6.72; staff rated morale at 5.36. Among editors, this marked a slip from their 1982 rating of 6.91; among staff, this showed a slight increase over their 1982 rating of 5.31 (see table 1).

Table 1 Editors' and staff members' perceptions of morale, 1982 and 2005

		1982 survey	2005 survey
Editors		6.91	6.72
Staff		5.31	5.36
	Difference	1.60	1.36

Remember this rating does not separately gauge editors' and staff members' morale but is a measure of each group's perception of newsroom-wide moral. Considering this, the most significant thing about the movement of the respective means may not be that editors are seeing a grumpier newsroom while staffers are experiencing a more optimistic one, but rather that editors' and staff members' perceptions are inching—slowly—toward alignment.

Despite this convergence, the disparity between editors' and staff members' perceptions of morale remains strong at papers where jobs have been cut. Layoffs and/or reductions in force affect morale much more than editors realize. On a scale of 1 to 10, staff at papers that had seen layoffs in the previous year rated morale at a paltry 3.77. Editors at those papers, secure in their jobs and perhaps wearing rose-colored glasses, rated newsroom morale 75 percent higher at 6.61 (see table 2).

Table 2 Perception of morale at newspapers that have had layoffs in the past 12 months, 2005

		Morale
Editors		6.61
Staff		3.77
	Difference	2.84

This trend also occurred at papers where there had been reductions in force in the past 12 months (see table 3).

Table 3 Perception of morale at newspapers that have had a reduction in force in the past 12 months, 2005

	Morale
Editors	5.96
Staff	4.80
Difference	1.16

This phenomenon was seen in the aforementioned case of the *Dallas Morning News.* When interviewing the paper's top management, Layton noted staff members were "concerned and puzzled" about how the layoff decisions were made.[6] Management's response? Layton said he "heard many words about going forward with a positive attitude. What I did not hear (and I listened hard for it) was anything resembling true regret, or a true comprehension of the pain that these men have inflicted. It sounded like salesmanship to me—good salesmanship, and persuasive in its way, but missing something vital."[7]

On the other side of the fence—the greener side, if you will—at newspapers where there have been no layoffs or reductions in force in the past 12 months, editors and staff were not only well above average in their morale ratings but also in closer alignment in their perception of newsroom morale (see table 4).

Table 4 Perception of morale at newspapers that have not had layoffs or a reduction in force in the past 12 months, 2005

Editors	7.11
Staff	6.13
Difference	0.98

---

6. Charles Layton, "The Dallas Mourning News."
7. Ibid.

We know then that newspapers that have seen recent layoffs are experiencing the lowest morale, but what exactly makes for a happy newsroom? While there isn't a one-size-fits-all formula for keeping the designers delighted, the copy editors content and the reporters living the life of Riley, there are some indicators of where the happiest journalists are likely to be.

One interesting measure examined in the 2005 survey was how often newsrooms discuss various ethical issues: news gathering methods, protection of sources, invasion of privacy, economic temptations, coverage of government secrecy and civil disorder, use of photographs, pressure from advertisers, fairness, conflicts of interest, use of reporters for non-news tasks, suppression of news, plagiarism and fabrication. Respondents were asked to rate the frequency with which such subjects were discussed, from never to several times a week. An index of responses to the 14 discussion-oriented questions included in the survey had a high degree of inter-correlation. This means that the questions all measure the same underlying characteristic: a chatty newsroom. Newsrooms can then be categorized into low discussion (lowest through 2.4396), medium discussion (2.43961 through 3.2143) and high discussion (3.21431 through highest). With this new measure, we can examine the impact of level of discussion on morale. (see table 5).

Table 5 Level of discussion and morale in newsrooms, 2005[a]

	Low discussion	Medium discussion	High discussion
Above-average morale	71%	65%	62%
Below-average morale	29	35	38

[a] Based on responses from editors

In newsrooms that rate high on the discussion index, morale was more likely, by 9 percentage points, to be below average than in those newsrooms with low discussion levels.[8] At papers where ethical dis-

---

8. Morale ratings from 1 to 6 are considered below average. Morale ratings from 7 to 10 are considered above average. One might be tempted to say, "Well, 6 seems pretty high on a scale of 1 to 10," but this break was determined by the mean.

cussions are the rarest, morale is highest. This result lends support to our assumption that a high level of discussion is an indicator of a problem.

Smaller papers probably take fewer risks and therefore have newsrooms with less to talk about. We can verify that discussion of ethical problems is more frequent in the newsrooms of larger circulation newspapers. Their frequency, as measured by the discussion index, is shown in Table 6.

Table 6 Level of ethical discussion by circulation size, 2005

	Small (circ. 50,000 or less)	**Medium** (circ. 50,001– 250,000)	**Large** (circ. 250,001 or more)
High discussion	35%	36%	57%
Medium discussion	37	34	29
Low discussion	27	30	15
Total	100%	100%	100%

We also know that circulation size plays a role in morale (see table 7). Staff perception of morale is lower at the larger papers, representing a significant difference among the groups. Editor perception is a little murkier, with the highest morale at the largest papers.

Table 7 Mean morale by newspaper circulation, 2005

	Editors	**Staff**
Small (circ. 50,000 or less)	6.75	5.63
Medium (circ. 50,001 – 250,000)	6.65	5.59
Large (250,001 or more)	6.79	4.91
Average	6.72	5.36

So if we know that discussion tends to increase with circulation and morale tends to decrease with circulation, we must isolate the effect from circulation to determine if discussion is actually influencing morale (as seen in table 5). A three-way crosstab allows us to do just that (see table 8). For the sake of consistency, we rely on editors' perceptions of both morale and discussion level. What we get is an interaction effect.

Table 8 Influence of discussion index on morale by circulation, 2005

	Low discussion	Medium discussion	High discussion
Small (circ. 50,000 or less)			
Above-average morale	58%	63%	65%
Below-average morale	42	37	35
Medium (circ. 50,001 – 250,000)			
Above-average morale	70%	67%	60%
Below-average morale	30	33	40
Large (circ. 250,001 or more)			
Above-average morale	100%	64%	61%
Below-average morale	0	36	39

This evidence shows that the relationship between discussion and morale boosting is reversed at the smaller papers. The more talk, the happier the newsroom. Small-town journalists are closer, both emotionally and socially, to their audiences, and vigorous discussion of ethical issues might be more beneficial for their own mental health. Other possible indicators of morale that can be gleaned from the 2005 survey include ownership and industry experience. Let's look at each of those in turn.

Drilling down on the principle of ownership, the 1982 and 2005 surveys included the following yes or no question,

> As you know, some newspaper companies are privately owned, and some are at least partly owned by investors who buy and sell stock on public exchanges. Do you think that whether a company is publicly or privately owned makes any difference in the way it serves its local community?

According to editors and staff members, ownership matters, and their perception of its influence is growing (see table 9).

Table 9 Impact of public or private ownership on service to local community, 1982 and 2005

	Editors		Staff	
	1982	**2005**	**1982**	**2005**
Makes a difference	38%	54%	39%	60%
No difference	62	46	61	40
Total	100%	100%	100%	100%

In 1982, editors and staff members were nearly even in their assessment of how ownership affects newspapers, a roughly 60-40 split among both groups that favored no difference. By 2005, those numbers had reversed for staff, and editors agreed that ownership matters. This could be attributable to the no-layoff policies some privately held newspapers have, higher salaries or simply less short-term pressure on the bottom line.

Of the respondents who said ownership made a difference in 2005, the majority of both editors and staff members said that the pressures of being publicly owned often or sometimes hinder a newspaper's ability to serve the local community (see table 10).

Table 10 Frequency of public ownership hindering a newspaper's ability to serve its community, 2005[a]

	Editors	Staff
Often	31%	28%
Sometimes	46	55
Rarely	11	14
Never	12	3
Total	100%[b]	100%[b]

[a] Respondents who said ownership made a difference only.
[b] Percents do not add to 100 due to rounding.

Beyond this, evidence has also become clear that ownership status has an impact on newsroom morale. In 1982, editors and staff members at publicly held newspapers rated newsroom morale higher than their private counterparts; by 2005, the situation had reversed (see table 11). Today, both editors and staff members at privately owned newspapers rate morale higher than their counterparts at publicly held newspapers, and the difference in ratings is greater than it was in 1982.

Table 11 Mean morale based on newspaper ownership, 1982 and 2005

		Editors		Staff	
		1982	2005	1982	2005
Private		6.93	6.83	5.29	5.55
Public		6.99	6.63	5.53	5.18
	Difference	−0.06	0.20	−0.24	0.37

There are plenty of factors that might have contributed to this shift. First, more newspapers are publicly held today than in 1982. Second, competition from cable television and the Internet have added to profit pressures for companies that have to worry about shareholders. Third, as we saw above, layoffs and reductions in force dramatically affect morale, and some privately held companies have no-layoff policies for their full-time employees. Even since the administration of this survey in the summer of 2005, ownership shake-ups and stakeholder-driven drama have underlined the extra burdens carried by publicly held news organizations.

The final measure we'll look at here is how work experience informs journalists' morale. Here we find a similar pattern among editors and staff (see table 12).

Table 12 Mean morale by years of experience in the newspaper business, 2005

	Editors	Staff
0 to 10	7.00	5.42
11 to 20	6.83	5.26
21 to 30	6.51	5.30
31 to 40	6.76	5.51
More than 40	7.42	5.50

Perception of morale is relatively high in the first decade of both editor and staff careers. Then it declines for the next two decades before turning around and reaching its highest point in the fifth decade.

Perhaps disillusionment sets in at mid-career, and only the congenitally happy are still around for four or five decades.

Other than the obvious reasons for both newly minted, fresh-faced editors and staff and their retirement-anticipating counterparts to rate morale higher, there may be other factors in play. Again, we have seen that layoffs and reductions in force dramatically affect morale. Younger employees don't earn as much in salary, so they may be more immune to budget-induced layoffs. Similarly, long-term employees may be among the more decorated and secure in their positions. The folks who have been in the business for a more moderate time span may feel less secure in their job status.

Conclusion

Morale is a tricky thing to measure. It depends on many different factors, and, as this paper clearly shows, it is subject to wildly different interpretations within the same newsroom. Furthermore, when measured, reports of morale are often counterintuitive. Staffers see morale peaking at small papers and reaching its nadir at the largest papers, for example. This report is by no means a comprehensive look at morale, and it is perhaps hindered by asking people to rate morale in their newsrooms rather than inquiring about personal job satisfaction. Nevertheless, these findings should indicate to editors that they need to pay more attention to factors that have a clearly detrimental effect on staff morale, such as layoffs, and that their outlook is perhaps overly positive. If a survey in another quarter-century finds editors and staff even more closely aligned in their assessment of morale, that will suggest progress.

CHAPTER 4

News Gathering:
On Shaky Ground?

Erik Holmes

Newspapers have become more reluctant to consider using controversial news-gathering techniques. This study shows that deceptive reporting tools such as false identities, stolen documents, concealed recording and eavesdropping are discussed and considered in newsrooms much less frequently in 2005 than in 1982.

This should not be surprising, as several recent controversies have shown that editors and publishers are increasingly skittish about tactics that appear even the slightest bit dishonest. For example, take the Jim DeFede case discussed in Chapter 1. The popular *Miami Herald* columnist was fired in July 2005 for taping, without consent, his conversation with former Miami city commissioner Arthur Teele Jr. just minutes before Teele committed suicide in the *Herald*'s lobby. Teele knew DeFede was a reporter—the two spoke frequently and were friends—but he did not know he was being recorded. This would be legal in many states, which only require that one party know about such recording, but it *can* be illegal in Florida.

DeFede told *USA Today* that he began taping not with intent to deceive or to capture a story, but as an impulse when he recognized the desperation in Teele's voice.[1] He said that he simply wanted a record of the frantic call.[2] Immediately after learning of Teele's suicide,

---

1. Peter Johnson, "Newspaper Criticized for Firing Columnist," *USA Today* (Aug. 1, 2005) http://www.usatoday.com/life/columnist/mediamix/2005-08-01-media-mix_x.htm (accessed Dec. 26, 2005).
2. Siobhan Morrissey, "A Suicide and a Dismissal," *Time* (Aug. 4, 2005) http://www.time.com/time/nation/printout/0,8816,1089923,00.html (accessed Dec. 26, 2005).

DeFede informed his editors of the recorded conversation. Within hours, he was fired.

Muckraking or subterfuge, this was not. But, then again, this is a different day than when Upton Sinclair, or even Woodward and Bernstein, were in newsrooms. Fiedler addressed the issue in an interview with *Time*: "The decision that I made clearly was guided by the environment in which we are operating today. I think that environment is much more constrained in terms of the latitude we give ourselves in our behavior—post-Jayson Blair. Maybe that's the line of demarcation."[3]

Have standards of acceptable news-gathering practices changed so much? How did we get to a climate in which a popular columnist at a major newspaper can be fired simply for tape-recording a conversation, a practice that Philip Meyer argues is akin to perfectly effective note-taking?[4] Have the media just lost their gumption? Are editors and publishers scared of bad publicity and lawsuits? And, most importantly, will timidity in news-gathering cause the media to forsake their sacred mission of shining light into dark places and serving as an independent "fourth estate?"

This chapter seeks to shed light on these issues by examining the recent evolution of news-gathering standards, practices and attitudes as reflected in popular, scholarly and trade media and in the 2005 survey.

Background

The old days of journalistic sting operations and intrigue seem to be pretty much in the past. A quick read of Meyer's anecdotes about risky ploys and colorful characters is striking because so little of this sexy culture exists in newsrooms today.[5]

There is limited empirical support for the widespread belief that newsrooms have become increasingly conservative in their news-gathering practices and attitudes. The only study examining the issue was

---

3. Ibid.
4. Meyer, *Ethical Journalism*, 81.
5. Ibid., 78–79.

Meyer and David Arant's 1996 follow-up to Meyer's 1982 study of journalism ethics.[6] The studies posed to newspaper editors and staffers a hypothetical scenario in which a reporter sneaks a hidden tape recorder into a closed meeting of a presidential candidate. In 1982, respondents representing 44 percent of newspaper circulation said the editor should kill the story and admonish the reporter; in 1996, that percentage had increased to 65 percent. This finding indicates that, as expected, newsrooms had grown increasingly reluctant to use controversial news-gathering techniques.

Meyer argued that the turning point at which deception and other controversial techniques became less acceptable was the shocking revelations of the Watergate investigation. As Ben Bradlee, executive editor of the *Washington Post*, said, "In a day in which we are spending thousands of man hours uncovering deception, we simply cannot deceive."[7] The Mirage bar incident in 1977, just a few years after Watergate, indicated that stricter rules now applied. The *Chicago Sun-Times* was disqualified from consideration for a Pulitzer Prize because undercover reporters on the story had opened a bar as a front from which to uncover bribery and fraud in city authorities.[8] A scheme that a few years before might have been lauded for its daring and creativity was now considered unethical by the journalistic powers that be.

Since the early 1990s, much of the debate regarding appropriate news-gathering methods has moved from the newsroom to the courtroom. Libel suits have proved extremely difficult for plaintiffs to win in the United States, so plaintiffs' attorneys have sought and found other successful avenues to challenge the behavior of the media— what *Chicago Tribune* lawyer Dale Cohen has called "trash torts." These include breach of contract, promissory estoppel, tortious interference, nuisance, unjust enrichment, stalking, negligence, fraud, trespass and invasion of privacy, among others.[9]

---

6. David M. Arant and Philip Meyer, "Changing Values in the Newsroom," *Nieman Reports* (Fall 1997): 57.

7. Meyer, 79.

8. Ibid.

9. Margaret Gorzkowski, "Focus on News-Gathering," *Quill* (Dec. 1998): 5–8.

There have been several important cases recently that have served to encourage the use of "trash torts" and embolden those who feel wronged by the media. A North Carolina jury in 1996 found ABC guilty of fraud, trespass and failure of duty of loyalty to an employer when it planted two reporters as Food Lion employees and used hidden cameras to uncover unsanitary meat-handling practices. In 1999, the *Cincinnati Enquirer* paid Chiquita Foods a reported $14 million out-of-court settlement and published a front-page apology after it was revealed that a reporter had illegally tapped into the company's voicemail system to gather information for a damaging exposé about questionable business practices. And in 1999, the U.S. Supreme Court sided with a plaintiff who challenged on Fourth Amendment grounds the long-standing practice of media entering suspects' homes with police during raids and arrests (ride-alongs).[10]

Gorzkowski argues that this trend represents something larger and more worrisome than judicial hostility: genuine public backlash. "What the media executive and the beat reporter must realize is that the public, as represented by recent juries, has chosen to punish journalistic violations of civil law," she writes.[11] As part of the broader decline in media credibility, a 1999 survey conducted for ASNE found that 80 percent of the American public believes that "journalists chase sensational stories because they think it'll sell papers, not because they think it's important news."[12] Rosemary Armao argues that journalists are in part to blame for this perception by employing controversial techniques such as hidden cameras for purely sensational stories, such as an expose on football star Michael Irvin's party life.[13] In light of such questionable judgment, it is little wonder that the public is reluctant to allow journalists to bend the rules.

---

10. Ibid.

11. Gorzkowski, "Focus on News-Gathering."

12. American Society of Newspaper Editors, "Examining Our Credibility: Perspectives of the Public and the Press," (Aug. 1999), http://www.asne.org/kiosk/reports/99reports/1999examiningourcredibility/p51-53_chasing.html (accessed Dec. 26, 2005).

13. Rosemary Armao, "Covert Newsgathering Tactics: Debating Deceptions," *IRE Journal* (Jan.–Feb. 1997): 3.

The turn of the public-opinion and judicial tides against the media has had a chilling effect on aggressive news-gathering tactics, some argue. After the massive Chiquita settlement, for example, Gannett Co. Inc., the nation's biggest newspaper publisher and owner of the *Cincinnati Enquirer*, distributed a company-wide memo reminding reporters and editors of the company's rules of conduct.[14] Asked if ABC would be willing to undertake a project similar to the Food Lion investigation again, ABC spokeswoman Eileen Murphy said, "It would be a lengthy conversation. We would have to consider how important [the story is] and the risks of going forward."[15]

First Amendment attorney Gary Bostwick of Bostwick & Hoffman in Santa Monica, Calif., framed the concern this way: "Lawyers are getting involved in the [news-gathering] process earlier and earlier on than they would have otherwise.... Before, the editor could handle a [news-gathering] situation from their experience.... Now it has become a legal dialog. And once that happens ... you have to pick up a phone and call your lawyer."[16]

Have these concerns in fact chilled journalists' willingness to use aggressive tactics to get the story? How have attitudes toward controversial news-gathering techniques changed in America's newsrooms since the era of "trash torts" began 15 years ago? Data collected in the 2005 ASNE survey may shed light on the subject.

The Changing Practice of News-Gathering

The subject of news-gathering is approached in the 2005 survey primarily via one question, which asks editors and staffers how often news-gathering methods ("using false identity; stolen documents;

---

14. Jim Moscou, "News-Gathering Tactics on Trial," *Editor & Publisher* (Dec. 18, 1999): 18–23.

15. Jim Moscou, "Court Flips Food Lion in Favor of ABC: Appeals Ruling Is a Setback for Wielding News-Gathering Torts against Journalists," *Editor & Publisher* (Oct. 23, 1999): 4–5.

16. Jim Moscou, "Legal Eagle's-Eye View of New Era," *Editor & Publisher* (Dec. 18, 1999): 26.

concealed recording; eavesdropping") are discussed at the respondent's paper. The identical question was asked in the 1982 survey, allowing for comparisons over time. Respondents were asked to choose from the following options: never, less than once a year, about once or twice a year, several times a year, about once a month, two or three times a month, nearly every week or several times a week. For analysis purposes, the data were combined into the following categories: less than once a year or never, from once a year to several times per year, and monthly or more often.

The data indicate that controversial news-gathering methods are discussed less frequently in 2005 than in 1982 (see table 1). In 1982, editors representing 28 percent of circulation said the issue was discussed less than once a year or never in their newsrooms, compared to 57 percent in 2005.

Table 1 Discussion of news-gathering methods in newsrooms, 1982 and 2005[a]

	1982	2005
At least monthly	8%	9%
Up to several times a year	64	35
Less than once a year or never	28	57
	100%	100%

[a] Editors only

The notable shift in responses allows us to conclude that news-gathering methods are less frequently discussed in newsrooms in 2005 than in 1982.

There were significant differences in the perceptions of editors and staffers with regard to the frequency of discussion of news-gathering (see table 2). Generally, editors were inclined to report a higher frequency of discussion than staffers.

Staffers representing 29 percent of newspaper readers responded that news-gathering is discussed once a year or more compared to editors representing 44 percent. This is in keeping with the logical assumption that bosses in general might perceive the work environments they oversee to be more dynamic and healthy—more

Table 2 Editors' and staff members' perceptions of news-gathering discussion, 2005

	Editors	Staff
Less than once a year or never	57%	71%
Up to several times per year	35	26
At least monthly	9	3
	100%	100%

discussion—than do their employees. Also, editors are in a position to be involved in more of those discussions.

Analysis of additional data collected in the 2005 ASNE survey allows us to describe some general characteristics of newspapers that discuss news-gathering and those that do not.

First, newsrooms that have a written policy on the use of anonymous sources were more likely to discuss news-gathering (see table 3). Among those who reported having a written anonymous source policy, respondents representing 36 percent of readers said they discuss news-gathering at least once per year to several times per year, compared to only 22 percent for those without such a policy.

Table 3 Anonymous source policies and discussion of news-gathering, 2005

	Source policy	No source policy
Less than once a year or never	59%	70%
Up to several times per year	36	22
At least monthly	5	8
Total	100%	100%

This suggests that, rather than stifle discussion, addressing ethical issues with a formal policy actually correlates with more robust discussion. However, the data does not address whether such policies contribute to creating discussion-oriented cultures.

There is also strong evidence that newsrooms in which there is more discussion of news-gathering methods have higher morale (see table 4). This was a strong relationship equating more talk with more morale.

Among papers in which news-gathering is regularly discussed, respondents representing 70 percent of circulation said morale was high

Table 4 Newsroom morale and discussion of news-gathering, 2005

	Discussion of news-gathering		
	Less than once a year or never	**Up to several times per year**	**At least monthly**
Above-average morale	47%	53%	70%
Below-average morale	53	47	30
	100%	100%	100%

in their newsrooms, compared to only 47 percent for those reporting that news-gathering was never or rarely discussed. This lends support to the encouraging idea that journalists appreciate a work environment in which they discuss important ethical issues.

The circulation of the newspaper also is correlated with the frequency of news-gathering discussion in the newsroom (see table 5). Small papers had the lowest level of discussion, with respondents representing 68 percent of circulation reporting that they discuss news-gathering tactics less than once a year or never, compared to 59 percent for large papers. Also, large newspapers were much more likely than small or medium-sized papers to discuss news-gathering methods at least monthly. Large newspapers representing 12 percent of that category's circulation reported regular discussion, compared to only 3 percent for small and medium-sized newspapers.

Table 5 Discussion of news-gathering methods and circulation, 2005

	Circulation		
	Small (circ. 50,000 or less)	**Medium** (circ. 50,001– 250,000)	**Large** (circ. 250,001 or more)
Less than once a year or never	68%	64%	59%
Up to several times per year	28	34	30
At least monthly	3	3	12
	100%[a]	100%	100%[a]

[a] Percents do not add to 100 due to rounding.

Both trends are logical. The smallest newspapers might not have the resources or time to engage in such discussions, and large newspapers might frequently cover important and sensitive enough topics that discussions of controversial news-gathering techniques would be necessary.

Conclusion

Our ability to draw conclusions from the data is limited by imperfections in the measurement instrument. The 2005 questionnaire included only one question related to news-gathering methods, compared to several on the 1982 questionnaire. Also, the data do not provide a direct measure of newspapers' willingness to use controversial news-gathering methods. The question instead asks about the frequency of discussions of methods.

However, we can assume from experience that a discussion of controversial news-gathering techniques is more likely to arise when the use of such techniques is being considered. Therefore, the reduced frequency of newsroom discussions is a likely indicator of reduced frequency of the actual use of controversial news-gathering techniques in 2005 as compared to 1982.

Because aggressive news-gathering techniques are sometimes essential for covering important stories and are increasingly under attack, it is imperative that we gain a better understanding of the prevailing attitudes and practices regarding the use of those techniques. There are no studies that systematically document the state of the newsroom in this regard, leaving ample opportunity for researchers to go beyond "discussion" and find out what techniques journalists actually use in their work and why they do or do not use them.

CHAPTER 5

FADING FREEDOM: THE CHANGING ROLE OF OMBUDSMEN

Jonathan Bloom

Today's newspaper ombudsmen are less independent than those of two decades ago. They are increasingly chosen by editors and required to submit their columns for approval. This reduced autonomy is troubling if you agree with Meyer, who wrote in 1987, "The key to the ombudsman's function is independence."[1] That is the reason many papers have or have had their ombudsmen sit away from the newsroom and the *Washington Post* hires its ombudsmen as independent contractors.[2]

It used to be rare for an ombudsman's column to be reviewed. Today, it's commonplace. In 1992, the editor of the *Winnipeg Free Press* demanded a prepublication review of ombudsman Barry Mullin's column. Mullin resigned in protest, claiming his independence would be compromised.

Losing Independence

In 1982, editors representing 37 percent of the circulation of newspapers with ombudsmen read their ombudsman's column before it ran. Today, that percentage has increased to 53. Further, when the column is read, editors representing 22 percent of the circulation of newspapers with ombudsmen read it for approval—as opposed to information—in 2005 compared with a scant 11 percent in 1982.

---

1. Meyer, *Ethical Journalism*, 166.
2. Lucia Moses, "Is There a Doctor in the House? Interestingly, Newspapers Call on Ombudsmen to Cure What Ails Them," *Editor & Publisher* (Jan. 10, 2000): 22–26.

This study also found that editors, not other newspaper leaders, choose a higher proportion of today's ombudsmen. In 1982, the selection of ombudsmen was done by editors representing 64 percent of the circulation of papers with ombudsmen, compared to 86 percent in 2005.

Then again, the news isn't all bad. More newspaper readers are represented by ombudsmen today. The number of ombudsmen belonging to their professional association has risen after a brief dip in the 1990s and the percentage of American newspaper readers with an ombudsman – as defined and reported by editors – increased from 1982 to 2005. Editors representing 20 percent of U.S. newspaper circulation reported having a regular ombudsman column, up from 15 percent in 1982, the result of some larger papers creating the position.

Most published research on this topic takes membership in the Organization of News Ombudsmen as the definition of the universe of ombudsmen.[3] But editors have a broader definition. In the 2005 survey, 34 editors answered yes to the question, "Does your newspaper have a regular ombudsman column?" and 15 of those papers did not have an ONO member on the staff. The majority of these (9 of the 15) had daily circulation less than 100,000.

Perhaps some editors responding to the ASNE surveys are defining themselves as the ombudsmen. Journalist Jennifer Dorroh interviewed editors at small and large papers, leading to her brief qualitative work "Who Needs One," a sidebar to her Ombudsman Puzzle. She found that editors at smaller papers have an easier time serving the ombudsman role, but that they benefit just as much from being accountable because they are intricately tied to the community.[4] James Ettema and Theodore Glasser's 1987 survey reached all but one of the then existing ONO members, and it yielded hard data on the characteristics of their newspapers, including their size. They reported that

---

3. For example, James S. Ettema and Theodore L. Glasser, "Public Accountability or Public Relations? Newspaper Ombudsmen Define Their role." *Journalism Quarterly* (Spring 1987) pp 3–12.

4. Jennifer Dorroh, "Who Needs One?" *American Journalism Review* (Feb./Mar. 2005): 50.

88 percent of ONO members worked at papers with circulation larger than 100,000. That has not changed very much. A check of the 34 papers listed on the ONO web site in January 2006 showed that 91 percent had more than 100,000 daily circulation.

Stable as that number might be, the ASNE survey indicates that the work of the ombudsman is shifting at some papers, adding even more treachery to what has already been known as a thankless job.

Background

Washington Post style columnist Gene Weingarten observed the work and interactions of that paper's ombudsman, Michael Getler, and made the following observation: "In my experience, most people feel he's almost always right, except when he's talking about them. Then he's blitheringly wrong."[5]

In the face of such double standards and usual newsroom ostracism, ideally ombudsmen give readers an advocate, open lines of communication within a newspaper and usually pen a column discussing their publication's performance and decisions. Why is it then, that so few daily papers in the United States have ombudsmen?[6] We know that ombudsmen have a strong history at our nation's newspapers.

Ombudsman is a Swedish word that derives from the Old Norse word *umbodhsmadhr*.[7] The word meant "the man who sees to it that the snow and ice and rubbish are removed from the streets and the chimneys are swept."[8] And since 1967, ombudsmen have been clean-

---

5. David Markiewicz, "Mike'll Get Ya: Michael Getler Has Proven To Be the Toughest Ombudsman at the *Washington Post* in a Long Time. What's the Impact of a Hard-Hitting In-House Critic on a Newspaper?" *American Journalism Review* (Nov. 2001): 64.

6. Kenneth Starck and Judy Eisele, "Newspaper Ombudsmanship as Viewed by Ombudsmen and Their Editors," *Newspaper Research Journal* (Fall 1999): 38.

7. *American Heritage College Dictionary,* 3rd ed. (Boston: Houghton Mifflin, 1993): 952.

8. Arthur Nauman. "News Ombudsmanship: Its History and Rationale," (paper presented at the symposium entitled "Press Regulation: How Far Has It Come?" Seoul, Korea, June 1994): 2.

ing up problems at American newspapers. We'll have to go back a few years, though, to find the word's first appearance in modern times. It acquired its current usage in Sweden in the realm of government. First appointed in 1809, ombudsmen were Swedish public officials who investigated complaints against their government.[9]

In 1916 Sweden applied the concept to the media, by creating the Swedish Press Council, or "Court of Honor," to provide a means for press self-discipline.[10] In 1922, a Japanese newspaper—Tokyo's *Asahi Shimbum*—followed suit and appointed a committee to hear reader complaints.

In the United States, Ralph Pulitzer established a Bureau of Accuracy and Fair Play at the *New York World* in 1913 as a reaction against the era of yellow journalism.[11] By the 1940s, there were calls for the press to regulate itself in response to credibility problems or face the prospect of being regulated by the government.[12] In 1947, *Time/Life* founder Henry Luce convened a group of non-journalists to examine the media. Named after its chairman, University of Chicago President Robert Maynard Hutchins, it was called the Hutchins Commission on Freedom of the Press.

At its close, the commission, which was supported by private philanthropy, issued a warning: the press either must monitor itself or risk being monitored by the government. "One of the most effective ways in improving the press is blocked by the press itself. By a kind of unwritten law, the press ignores the errors and misrepresentations, the lies and the scandals, of which its members are guilty," the Commission wrote.[13]

The Hutchins Commission's ideas were largely ignored by the mainstream press and the idea didn't catch on in the United States until 1967. That year, two separate magazine articles called for news-

---

9. Moses, "Is There a Doctor in the House?"
10. Ibid., 3.
11. Cassandra Tate, "What Do Ombudsmen Do? Some Editors Think a Readers' Advocate Is a Bummer. But 36 Papers Are Trying It Out," *Columbia Journalism Review* (May/June 1984): 37.
12. Nauman, "News Ombudsmanship," 3.
13. Ibid.

papers to create ombudsmen positions. In the March issue of *Esquire*, Ben Bagdikian, a longtime *Washington Post* staffer, pushed for ombudsmen to represent the public on newspapers' boards of directors.[14] A.H. Raskin, writing in the June 11, 1967, issue of the *New York Times Magazine*, proposed a department of internal criticism headed by an ombudsman to reverse declining reader confidence in newspapers.[15]

In June 1967, the same month Raskin's article appeared, Norman Isaacs, editor of Louisville's *Courier Journal*, named the first American newspaper ombudsman. He appointed former city editor John Herchenroeder to handle complaints, but not write a column.[16]

In 1970, the *Washington Post* established the second U.S. ombudsman and many other papers followed suit. By 1980, there were enough newspaper ombudsmen around to warrant the formation of the ONO. With a brief dip in the mid 1990s, the number of ombudsmen has hovered near 35 since the mid 1980s (see figure 1).

The *New York Times*, the standard by which most American newspapers measure themselves, long eschewed the idea of an ombudsman, despite Raskin's wishes. In the wake of the 2003 Jayson Blair scandal, however, many wondered whether an ombudsman might have helped prevent that embarrassment.[17] The *Washington Post* Executive Editor Ben Bradlee disagreed, saying that the *Post*'s ombudsman did nothing to prevent the Janet Cooke scandal in 1981.[18] Partly

---

14. Neil Nemeth and Craig Sanders, "Ombudsmen's Interactions with Public through Columns," *Newspaper Research Journal* (Winter 1999): 29–42 referencing Ben Bagdikian, "The American Newspaper Is Neither Record, Mirror, Journal, Ledger, Bulletin, Examiner, Register, Chronicle, Gazette, Observer, Monitor, Transcript nor Herald of the Day's Events," *Esquire* (March 1967): 124, 138, 142–144, 146.

15. Nemeth and Sanders, "Ombudsmen's Interactions with Public through Columns," referencing A.H. Raskin, "What's Wrong With American Newspapers?" *The New York Times Magazine* (July 11, 1967): 28, 83.

16. Philip Meyer, *The Vanishing Newspaper* (Columbia: University of Missouri Press, 2004): 172.

17. Neil Nemeth, *News Ombudsmen in North America* (Westport: Praeger, 2003): 143–144.

18. Ibid., 144.

Figure 1 Number of North American newspapers employing ombudsmen, 1967 to 2005

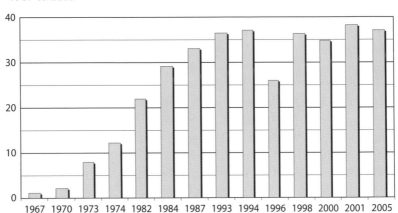

swayed by the Blair fallout, the *Times* finally hired an ombudsman in December 2003, naming author Daniel Okrent as its first public editor to both "make us more sensitive on matters of fairness and accuracy, and enhance our credibility," said *Times* Executive Editor Bill Keller.[19]

One other important moment for ombudsmen came in 1980. Robert Haiman, then the *St. Petersburg Times* executive editor and later head of the Poynter Institute, told ombudsman Dorothy Smiljanich to apologize after some staffers claimed that her column explaining why the paper sent only black reporters to cover a race riot was racist. After she resigned instead, Haiman eliminated the position and has since become an outspoken critic of ombudsmanship.[20]

With this rich history, academics, journalists, and, not surprisingly, ombudsmen, have written a decent amount about ombudsmanship. Much of the work, particularly earlier, examined just who

---

19. Jennifer Dorroh, "The Ombudsman Puzzle," *American Journalism Review* (Feb./Mar. 2005): 50.

20. Kate McKenna, "The Loneliest Job in the Newsroom," *American Journalism Review* (Mar. 1993): 43.

they were and what they did. On the former question, Ettema and Glasser's 1987 survey of North American ombudsmen found that their mean age was 55.4, older than the average age of publishers and editors. They were primarily male and had an average of 20 years editing and 10 years reporting experience. In short, they were crusty old newspapermen.

In examining the ombudsmen's role, a common theme was the duality of their position. Many scholars discussed how the ombudsmen's task was to both improve the journalism and accuracy while reaching out to readers. Neil Nemeth's book, *News Ombudsmen in North America*, theorized that ombudsmen improved accountability, solved disputes, and served as public relations officers for their newspapers.[21]

Several articles also focused on the public relations role of ombudsmen. When Ettema and Glasser surveyed ombudsmen, they found that they essentially performed a major public relations role. Yet, they did not view their role as PR.[22] Neil Nemeth and Craig Sanders content analyzed ombudsmen's columns and found that 85 percent of the nearly 20,000 coded paragraphs showed "purely public relations behavior."[23]

Scholars have written about why there are so few ombudsmen. Not surprisingly, money is a major factor. Many editors and publishers balk at the extra cost of hiring an ombudsman, especially because their experience and age make them well paid. Nemeth's 1999 survey of ombudsmen found that the average salary was between $75,000 and $100,000.[24] At smaller papers with weaker budgets, that expense just may not be feasible.

Some authors say, however, that the financial issue is merely a cover. *Seattle Times* ombudsmen Colleen Patrick was told that her contract was not renewed in 1992 as a cost-cutting move. She felt, however, that her "pro-active" approach had much to do with it.[25] Alex Jones, director of the Joan Shorenstein Center on the Press, Pol-

21. Nemeth, *News Ombudsmen in North America*, 142.

22. Ettema and Glasser, "Public Accountability or Public Relations?" 7

23. Neil Nemeth and Craig Sanders, "Ombudsmen's Interactions with Public through Columns," *Newspaper Research Journal* (Winter 1999): 29.

24. Dorroh, "The Ombudsman Puzzle," 52.

25. McKenna, "The Loneliest Job in the Newsroom," 42.

itics, and Public Policy at Harvard University said that publishers don't want to appoint ombudsmen unless they have to because ombudsmen anger reporters and editors.[26]

Another problem with ombudsmen about which many academics have written is that their presence reduces the editor's interaction with readers. Former *Times* Executive Editor A.M. Rosenthal argued that ombudsmen make editors lazy.[27] The *St. Louis Post-Dispatch* got rid of its reader representative in 2001 because Editor Ellen Soeteber felt that direct interaction with an editor was best. The *Washington Post*'s Bradlee finds that approach unrealistic. "It's a very cheap and easy shot to say that the editor should be the ultimate ombudsman ... but anybody who says he or she can manage to read everything that goes into that paper is kidding himself."

Nemeth, in a chapter of his book *News Ombudsmen in North America*, provided a more qualitative look at the experience of ombudsmen at small and medium-sized newspapers. He did so by providing an in-depth examination of ombudsmen's experiences at four smaller papers.

In his 2004 book *The Vanishing Newspaper*, Philip Meyer compared the retention of household penetration in the home county for newspapers with ombudsmen to competitors in similarly sized markets without one. He found that the 29 newspapers with ONO members in 1996 had retained 89.3 percent of home county circulation, while non-ombudsman papers retained 86.3 percent in the same five-year period.[28] While the difference wasn't massive, it was noteworthy and statistically significant. Meyer attributed that difference to the ombudsman being a visible sign to the community that a paper cares about its reputation and influence in the community and suggested that this care might be manifested in many other ways.

In another example of quantitative research on ombudsmen, a 1999 survey by Kenneth Starck and Julie Eisele asked ombudsmen and editors the same three questions—the ombudsman's most important

26. Dorroh, "The Ombudsman Puzzle," 52.
27. McKenna, "The Loneliest Job in the Newsroom," 42.
28. Meyer, *The Vanishing Newspaper*, 172.

duty, advantages, and disadvantages. The answers were mostly similar, except 27 percent of ombudsmen felt they enhanced the paper's credibility, compared to only 12 percent of editors.[29]

Furthermore, a 1986 study by researchers at San Diego State University found that most of the 350 readers surveyed were more satisfied with the *San Diego Union* because it had an ombudsman.[30] And University of Iowa Professor Gil Cranberg's 1984 study of libel suits found that almost nine of ten libel plaintiffs said a negative response to their complaint encouraged them to sue.[31] Essentially, an ombudsman could provide an outlet for the hostility that generates many libel suits.

There is plenty of literature providing anecdotal evidence about the extent of ombudsmen's usefulness. For example, Arthur Nauman, the ombudsman at the *Sacramento Bee* from 1980 to 1997, told an audience at a June 1994 symposium in Seoul, Korea, that he has seen his presence motivate editors and reporters to produce more careful work.[32]

Contrastingly, Kate McKenna's article examined some of the objections to ombudsmen. She gave voice to Robert Haiman and former *Miami Herald* Executive Editor Douglas Clifton. They called ombudsmen "the worst thing you can do" when readers feel distanced and "a barrier" between the staff and readers, respectively.[33]

While many articles noted the objections to ombudsmen, a 2001 study by Nemeth and Sanders compared competing newspapers with and without ombudsmen and found ombudsmen provided "only a modest extension of dialogue between newspapers and their readers."[34] They coded correction boxes, letters to the editor, and ombudsmen columns and found that ombudsmen "constitute a truncated dialogue that is largely devoid of meaningful discussion about the newspaper's performance." [35]

---

29. Starck and Eisele, "Newspaper Ombudsmanship," 37–49.
30. McKenna, "The Loneliest Job in the Newsroom," 44.
31. Ibid., 44.
32. Arthur Nauman. "News Ombudsmanship," 5.
33. McKenna, "The Loneliest Job in the Newsroom," 43.
34. Neil Nemeth and Craig Sanders, "Meaningful discussion of performance missing," *Newspaper Research Journal*, (Winter 2001): 56.
35. Ibid., 55.

In contrast, there is a dearth of material providing a quantitative measure of ombudsmen's effects. Some of the existing scholarly work on ombudsmen has noted the difficulty in quantifying the impact of ombudsmen. And from a practitioner's perspective, Cassandra Tate's article noted that the *Boston Globe*, "in what can be interpreted as one way to quantify the work of its ombudsman, publishes an annual box score on corrections, listing the number and type that appeared during the year and comparing them with the previous year."[36]

More Changes

While we know from the 2005 data that the trend away from ombudsman independence is well under way, we still haven't pinpointed where and why. The 2005 survey found that editors of newspapers that are publicly held are more likely to read their ombudsman's column for approval rather than for information, as opposed to editors of newspapers that are privately held (see table 1).

Table 1 Editors read ombudsman's column for information or approval by ownership, 2005 [a]

	Private	Public
For information	72%	54%
For approval	28	46
Total	100%	100%

[a] Editors whose papers have an ombudsman's columns only

Even setting aside ownership, however, editors whose papers have an ombudsman's column on the whole are now more concerned with what their ombudsman writes than they were in 1982 (see table 2). This lack of independence is not a positive sign for readers who look to the ombudsman as a neutral inside-the-newsroom representative. But what does it mean for the newsroom?

---

36. Tate, "What Do Ombudsmen Do?" 41.

Table 2 Editors read ombudsman's column for information or approval, 1982 and 2005 [a]

	1982	2005
For information	89%	64%
For approval	11	37
Total	100%	100% [b]

[a] Editors whose papers have an ombudsman's columns only
[b] Percents add to more than 100 due to rounding.

The 2005 survey did contain one other bright spot. According to the survey, the presence of an ombudsman at a paper does seem to affect the newsroom morale. At newspapers with ombudsmen, 80 percent of staff and editors had above average morale, compared to 63 at papers without ombudsmen. The presence of an ombudsman does not make papers more sensitive to ethical issues, though. In fact, it has almost no effect whatsoever on both topics.

Unlike in the past, having an ombudsman doesn't improve a newspaper's internal dialogue on ethical issues. The 2005 study showed that having an ombudsman is not linked to the amount of newsroom discussion. In 1982, however, they were. That year, 72 percent of staff and editors at newspapers with an ombudsmen said they talked about ethical issues several times a year or more, compared to 49 percent at papers without ombudsmen. The shift in this issue could be a result of newsroom staffs being stretched so thin that there isn't much time for discussion. Or, perhaps, ombudsmen's novelty has worn off at their papers.

Outlook for Ombudsmen

The number of ombudsmen has remained relatively stable and a higher percentage of editors representing newspaper circulation have ombudsmen. This is likely a result of more ombudsmen working at some larger papers and flies in the face of newspapers' cost-cutting measures. Papers may not want to abandon ombudsmen to save a few bucks. Meyer's 2004 report provided evidence that ombudsmen could justify their relatively high salaries with a higher reader retention rate.

As the ombudsman movement ages, some doubt remains over its effectiveness. Will the ombudsmen retain their independence and scrappiness or will the value of their work be undercut by editorial scrutiny? "There seems to be a growing feeling that ombudsmen are becoming enmeshed in this whole contemporary need to be of service to our readers," said Arthur Nauman. "What worries me is that process is taking the place of vigorous, fearless criticism of the journalistic product, not an analysis of how pretty the paper is."[37]

While there is not yet any published research on the topic, Web blogs and media Web sites like the one run by Jim Romenesko may reduce the usefulness of ombudsmen. Instead of calling or writing editors, readers with a gripe or compliment are able to post their feelings on the Web for the whole world to read. If blogs don't replace ombudsmen, they might take away some of their business.

---

37. Nemeth, *News Ombudsmen in North America*, 147.

CHAPTER 6

Newspapers and the Right to Privacy: New Rules?

Casey Ferrell

Newspaper newsrooms have become more sensitive to privacy issues in the past two decades—and also more confident in their ability to deal with them. Further, despite developing case law that makes invasion of privacy more of a risky business, the issue was discussed less in newsrooms in 2005 than it was in 1982. There are, however, some interesting findings that indicate certain aspects of privacy are now dealt with more delicately, running contrary to the industry ethos, "Publish, publish, always publish."

The fact that this issue is discussed less often in newsrooms is curious when one considers modern trends in privacy law. In general, privacy laws have become stricter. That is, it is easier for plaintiffs to claim their privacy has been invaded because new laws have lowered a plaintiff's burden of proof. Therefore, it would seem that invasion of privacy issues at newspapers would be more prevalent because the newspapers themselves are at greater risk of being successfully sued.

Legalese

In legal terms, invasion of privacy can be broken down into four torts: intrusion, disclosure of private facts, false light and misappropriation. Newspapers typically face lawsuits based on the first three torts, but are rarely sued for misappropriation.

Intrusion resembles the much older tort of trespass, and prohibits unauthorized entry into an area where a person has a reasonable expectation of privacy, whether or not such entry occurs for the ostensible purpose of gathering news. Intrusion is the only one of the four traditional invasion of privacy torts to which newsworthiness provides no defense.

For example, in the course of working on a story about the high salaries and extravagant lifestyles of some HMO executives, reporters for *Inside Edition* videotaped U.S. Healthcare chairman Leonard Abramson and his family at work and at home. The television crew rented a boat, anchored it in a public waterway outside the Abramsons' Florida estate, and used a camera equipped with a telephoto lens and a sensitive microphone to videotape the exterior of the house. Abramson's daughter and son-in-law sued the journalists for intrusion, and a federal district court in Philadelphia, despite recognizing the importance of news coverage of the HMO industry and the people who run it, ordered the *Inside Edition* crew to stop following and taping the subjects of their story.[1]

Intrusion covers invasive news gathering methods, and the well-known case involving Jim DeFede, also discussed in Chapters 1 and 4, illustrates just how fine the line is between what is legal and what is not. DeFede was fired for tape recording a conversation with a prominent politician, Arthur Teele Jr., who shortly after committed suicide in the paper's lobby. The *Miami Herald* argued that the tape recording was illegal, but there was no prosecution, and it remains unclear whether DeFede's actions were criminal. Nevertheless, this story illustrates the enormous impact that privacy law has on the routine operations of a newspaper and its staff.

Disclosure of private facts typically involves the public dissemination of information that is intimate, highly offensive and of no legitimate public concern. Unlike intrusion, newsworthiness is a defense to a private facts claim, and information of legitimate public concern may not serve as the basis for a private facts lawsuit. For example, the victim of a sexual assault in a jail in South Carolina sued a newspaper for printing his name in a story about the crime. The state Supreme Court ruled in favor of the newspaper because the crime was a matter of public significance.[2]

---

1. *Wolfson v. Lewis*, 168 F.R.D. 530 (E.D. Pa. 1996)
2. *Doe v. Berkeley Publishers*, 496 S.E.2d 636 (S.C. 1998)

The term private facts is undergoing an expansion of meaning. Medical information, for example, is now more protected than ever. Also, in several states, a person can opt out of having the information on his or her driver's license publicly available.

False light is much like libel, although the intent of this tort is compensate for the plaintiff's hurt feelings rather than the damage their reputations may suffer. Some states do not recognize false light as a privacy tort because of its close similarity to libel. In false light cases, plaintiffs must first prove that information published about them was in fact not true.[3] Because of this condition, newspapers can generally avoid lawsuits of this kind by printing only what they know to be factual information—a guiding principle of the industry. Therefore, false light suits rarely end in favor the plaintiff. The exception to this rule is in California, where celebrities often sue for false light and indeed sometimes prevail.

Misappropriation lawsuits hinge on whether the use of a person's name or image is intended for profit. News coverage, even when it includes the names and images of celebrities, is usually immune from misappropriation suits because its purpose is to provide information, rather than to promote the sale of a product or service.

The media are increasingly facing privacy lawsuits based not on the traditional privacy torts but on related claims such as fraud and intentional infliction of emotional distress.[4] This is an indication that privacy law is evolving, and the direction in which it's headed is to provide more and more protection to private citizens. This trend obviously puts newspapers at greater risk and requires them to be increasingly considerate of invasion of privacy issues.

Some of the most essential functions of the press are being inhibited by recent federal legislation. Limitations to access to public records have been enacted since the September 11, 2001, terrorist attacks thanks in part to provisions within the Patriot Act. It is now harder for journalists to obtain public documents and personally

---

3. Jane E. Kirtley, "The Privacy Paradox," *The News Media and the Law* (Spring 1999): 5.
4. Ibid., 15.

identifiable information through the use of the Freedom of Information Act. While it was never an easy or efficient process to begin with, journalists are being ever more stonewalled by federal restrictions to access.

Privacy Issues in the Newsroom

With the legal walls closing in, it would stand to reason that privacy issues would be a hot topic among editors and staff in newsrooms across the country. But this is not the case. In 1982, editors representing 39 percent of daily newspaper circulation in the United States said they discussed the issue of invasion at least monthly, whereas in 2005 that percentage dropped to 28 (see table 1).

Table 1 Discussion of invasion of privacy in newsrooms, 1982 and 2005[a]

	1982	2005
Less than once a year or never	5%	17%
Up to several times per year	57	55
At least monthly	39	28
	100%	100%

[a] Editors only

The conclusion is clear—invasion of privacy issues are simply less talked about in American newsrooms.

Predicting factors for this phenomenon are scarce. The findings remained constant despite taking into account factors such as private versus pubic ownership and staff versus editor responses. The one constant predictor of the level of discussion of invasion of privacy issues is the size of the newspaper. Editors and staff representing 26 percent of newspapers with circulations of 250,000 or more said the issue was discussed at least once a week, compared to only 4 percent at papers with a circulation less than 250,000. Larger newspapers, because of factors such as the sheer volume of reportage and frequent investigative projects, talk about invasion of privacy more often than small newspapers.

It would stand to reason that the presence of a code of ethics might affect how often privacy issues are discussed, perhaps by reducing the need for discussion because rules are clear. But surprisingly, whether a newspaper has a written code of ethics has no significant impact on the frequency of discussion.

And finally, in what is perhaps the biggest surprise, respondents' experience (or years in the newspaper business) also has no effect. Seasoned journalists, one might expect, would be the most prepared to handle the issue of invasion of privacy because their experience has taught them what is and is not permissible. That is, veteran reporters would discuss the issue less. To reverse the hypothesis, cub reporters could be expected to discuss the issue more often because they have questions about the law or about their newspaper's practices. Instead, the data suggest that journalists old and new are talking about privacy issues equally.

Beyond discussion, both surveys targeted another aspect of invasion of privacy, with the following question:

> A prominent citizen is vacationing alone in Key West, and his hotel burns down. The wire service story lists him among those who escaped uninjured and identifies the hotel as a popular gathering place for affluent gays. The citizen says he'll commit suicide if you publish his name in the story.
> Should the editor:
> (1) Publish in full
> (2) Publish the story, but without mentioning the gay angle
> (3) Publish the story, but without mentioning the prominent citizen
> (4) Kill the story

In 1982, editors representing 41 percent of newspaper readers said the story should be published in full, whereas in 2005 editors representing only 30 percent of daily newspaper circulation approved of publishing the story in full (see table 2). Staff members trended in the same direction, away from publishing the story in full. This finding indicates greater sensitivity on the part of newspapers when it comes to publishing embarrassing—or perhaps legally protected—personal facts about private citizens.

The two significant findings of this report at first blush don't seem to square with one another. Why would newspapers now be more

Table 2 Hypothetical invasion of privacy scenario, 1982 and 2005

	Editors		Staff	
	1982	**2005**	**1982**	**2005**
(1) Publish in full	41%	30%	46%	33%
(2) Publish without gay angle	52	59	43	49
(3) Publish without citizen's name	7	10	10	16
(4) Kill the story	0	0	0	1
	100%	100%a	100%a	100%a

a Percents do not add to 100 due to rounding.

sensitive toward certain privacy issues, such as publishing someone's sexual orientation, if the subject of privacy is generally talked about less? It would appear that there are two separate phenomena occurring. In newspaper newsrooms across the country, there seems to be a growing confidence about how to handle invasion of privacy issues, and this has led to a decline in how often the subject comes up in discussion. At the same time, news professionals are expressing greater sensitivity to the rights of citizens to keep certain personal information out of the public sphere.

There are some interesting implications for further research based on the results of the hypothetical ethical scenario posed by the Key West question above. First, the question relates to a specific private fact, homosexuality, that has undergone cultural and political changes since 1982. Perhaps homosexuality is not quite as newsworthy as it once was. Or perhaps because there is now greater awareness and possibly acceptance of homosexuality, those in the newspaper business are more inclined to believe that sexual orientation is a private fact that, if printed, may land them in legal trouble. Second, the question poses the threat of suicide. While no one wants the blood of a citizen on one's hands, this sentiment may be stronger now because of incidents like the DeFede case. In fact, the DeFede case could be a manifestation of greater sensitivity. Regardless of whether that is true, the suicide component of the question likely had an impact on respondents' answers to the scenario.

In further surveys, this particular question should be split into three separate scenarios: one that only addresses a citizen's sexual orientation; one that only addresses a citizen's suicide threat; and one that addresses a different private fact, such as a citizen's past substance abuse. In doing so, future research will be able to more specifically identify respondents' attitudes toward invasion of privacy and what kinds of personal information should be published.

Conclusion

Invasion of privacy is becoming an increasingly dicey issue for reporters and editors, and the drop-off in the discussion of this issue in newsrooms does not bode well for the industry. As mentioned, this trend might reflect a growing confidence on the part of news professionals, but confidence can rapidly lead to complacency. The legal ramifications of invading people's privacy during the course of newsgathering and news distribution should prompt editors around the country to address *more* thoroughly and *more* carefully their practices and guidelines, not less. As the number of lawsuits alleging invasion of privacy on behalf of newspapers continues to rise, the industry has demonstrated that it is becoming more sensitive to citizens' specific privacy rights. But unfortunately, this increased sensitivity has not resulted in broader newsroom communication about privacy. Raising awareness of the changing legal landscape of privacy could enable reporters and editors to make better decisions while simultaneously fostering a more communicative newsroom environment.

CHAPTER 7

DIVERSITY IN NEWSROOMS: A PATH TOWARD IMPROVEMENT?

Nicole Elise Smith

In 1978 the American Society of Newspaper Editors made a major commitment toward increasing discourse about *all* Americans. The commitment was to increase diversity in newsrooms across the country. The findings of this study indicate that the newspaper business is well on its way: there is a shrinking gender divide among newsroom employees, and newspaper employees are showing increased concern for reflecting community diversity. These positive findings show progress even though the initial goal set by ASNE in 1978 has not been met.

By the year 2000, ASNE hoped to have minority employment in newsrooms match minority representation in the U.S. population.[1] In 1998 when it was becoming clear that ASNE would not reach its original goal, the diversity mission was re-stated. The new mission aimed to have newsrooms reflect racial diversity in the population by 2025 or sooner.[2] The year 2000 goal was not met nor is it likely that newsroom diversity will reflect racial diversity in the American population by 2025. The annual 2005 ASNE survey found that only 13 percent of journalists in the United States were journalists of color, while minorities represented 33 percent of the U.S. population, according to the 2000 census.[3]

ASNE is just one of the journalism organizations to have contributed significant efforts toward reaching this goal. In fact, the Free-

---

1. "Building the Rainbow in Journalism," *The Forum* (July 1994): 4–7.
2. Ronald Roach, "Investigating Newsroom Diversity," *Black Issues in Higher Education* (Aug. 16, 2001): 19–26.
3. "Journalists of Color Work Toward Increasing Newsroom Diversity," *Black Issues in Higher Education* (May 5, 2005): 11.

dom Forum has included newsroom diversity among its top three priorities. In 2000 the Freedom Forum, in partnership with ASNE, dedicated $5 million toward achieving greater diversity in newsrooms.[4] The money was divided among numerous diversity initiatives, including recruiting and retaining minority journalists, scholarships, and professional development programs. In regard to the initiative, Charles Overby, CEO of the Freedom Forum, said, "We believe, for newspapers to be complete, fair and accurate, the makeup of their news staff should reflect the diversity of the nation."[5]

In 2002, the Freedom Forum launched a Diversity Directory, which is a database designed to help newspapers in increasing newsroom diversity through college recruiting.[6] The database contains information on more than 200 colleges and universities, including tribal and historically black universities.[7] Additionally, the Freedom Forum and APME are currently providing recruiting grants to small-newspaper editors to encourage use of the database.

Diversity efforts have also stemmed—both intentionally and unintentionally—from within newsrooms themselves. In 2001, the *Savannah Morning News* launched their "Neighborhood Newsroom."[8] In this program, local residents are recruited and given intensive journalism training. They are then asked to periodically submit articles of interest, with the hope that these new voices will bring varying viewpoints to the paper. Although the program has faced its own hurdles, it remains a dedicated internal effort toward increasing diversity. In early 1994, the *Spokesman-Review* launched a column called "Your Turn," designed to provide a forum for those people who felt they were normally overlooked in the newspaper.[9] Following one

---

4. "$5 Million Effort Seeks to Achieve More Diversity in Newspaper Newsrooms," *American Journalism Review* (May 2000): 20.

5. Ibid.

6. "Freedom Forum Launches Database to Aid Newsroom Diversity Efforts," *Black Issues in Higher Education* (Mar. 14, 2002): 21.

7. Ibid.

8. Steve Corrigan, "Wanted: Diversity of Voice and Experience," *Nieman Reports* (Spring 2001): 75–76.

9. G. Douglas Floyd, "A Sacrifice for Civic Journalism," *American Journalism Review* (July/Aug. 1997): 15.

"Your Turn" column written by Karen Boone, an African American woman who highlighted the "ethnic invisibility" that she faced, intense community debate ensued.[10] The debate turned quite heated and the *Spokesman-Review* took an active role in encouraging readers to become involved in "local human and civic rights activities." In an *American Journalism Review* article Douglas Floyd concluded that "the incident galvanized the community, and provided a fitting backdrop for a much-needed public discussion about racism."[11]

Despite these pointed and not so pointed efforts to increase diversity in newsrooms, setbacks have occurred. Following its launch in 1982, *USA Today* was viewed by many as a model for racial diversity in the newsroom. It had a high record for reporting racial diversity and was one of the first publications to hire minorities for decision-making positions.[12] However, *USA Today* came under fire in 1996 after it "eliminated" the position of Barbara Reynolds, essentially firing her. Reynolds was the only female African American columnist on the paper and the only African American member of the editorial board. Additionally, Reynolds was a highly respected journalist and known by many to "give voice to the voiceless," thereby highlighting racial and economic injustices.[13] While *USA Today* maintained that the elimination of Reynolds' position was actually an attempt to achieve greater diversity within the newspaper, critics maintained that Reynolds was fired because the newspaper was attempting to target a more affluent audience.[14]

The *New York Times* also has a proven track record in regard to diversity. However, the scandal surrounding the actions of Jayson Blair led to polarized positions about race in the newsroom. One side of the polarized debate "holds that race had nothing to do with the Blair affair, and to even bring it up is to somehow imply that Blair plagia-

---

10. Ibid.

11. Ibid.

12. Dorothy Gilliam, "Newspaper Silences a Special Voice," *Washington Post* (July 20, 1996): C01.

13. Ibid.

14. Norman Solomon, "*USA Today* Mutes a Challenging Voice," *EXTRA!* (Sept./Oct. 1996): 20.

rized and fabricated because he is black."[15] The other side maintains that "race had everything to do with it, and that Blair is exhibit A in the case against all deliberate attempts to diversify the workplace."[16] A 2003 unsigned editorial in *CJR* concluded that the need for diversity within newsrooms is crucial. Whatever position one takes in regard to Blair and diversity, the issue highlights the challenge and lack of discussion in regard to managing diversity, once it finds its way into newsrooms.[17]

Retention of minority journalists has also been a problematic issue. Additionally, many minority journalists have been at odds with their employers.[18] The more common complaints are that they are overlooked for the prestigious assignments and that they have difficulty getting promotions.[19] A 1993 study by the National Association of Black Journalists found that while 67 percent of African American journalists said that their managers were not committed to promoting and retaining minority journalists only 5 percent of managers agreed.[20]

As a solution to the diversity divide, some media researchers assert that until diversity is seen as part of the overall business strategy, it will continue to cause tensions in newsrooms.[21] Walterene Swanston argues that increasing diversity in newsrooms can bring about business advantages, such as reaching new readers and advertisers, attracting talent with diverse and fresh viewpoints, and an increase in productivity throughout the paper. A 2001 study that analyzed in-depth interviews with newspaper employees at the *Los Angeles Times* came to a similar conclusion. Although the researchers argued that it is too soon to draw definitive conclusions, their data indicated that

---

15. "Unfinished Business: As the Jayson Blair Debate Makes Clear, We Still Need Diversity Programs," *Columbia Journalism Review* (July/Aug. 2003): 7.

16. Ibid.

17. Ibid.

18. Roach, "Investigating Newsroom Diversity."

19. Ibid.

20. Ibid.

21. Walterene Swanston, "The *Post* and Racial Diversity: Racial Tensions Will Persist in America's Newsrooms Until Diversity Is Seen As a Business Strategy Rather Than Social Engineering," *American Journalism Review* (Nov. 1995): 16.

increased diversity among newspapers may lead to a rise in circulation.[22] In summarizing the situation, Swanston concluded, "Making sure diversity training is provided to everyone in a company will lead to broader acceptance, particularly if staffers realize that diversity makes good business sense."[23]

Diversity in Newsrooms

Gender diversity is improving. Specifically in 1982, editors representing 95 percent of daily newspaper circulation were male (see table 1). In 2005, the figure shifted to 79 percent.

Table 1 Editors' gender, 1982 and 2005

	1982	2005
Male	95%	79%
Female	5	21
Total	100%	100%

Increasing diversity across time was also seen among staff members. In 1982, staffers representing 69 percent of readers were male. By 2005, however, staff members representing only 55 percent of newspaper circulation were male. (The latter percent is based on the 91 percent of respondents for whom gender was known.)

Impact of Gender Diversity in the Newsroom

Although the increased gender diversity has fallen short of ASNE goals, the trend's impact on male and female editors is still worth examining. To begin to understand the effects of diversity in the news-

---

22. Richard Gross, Patricia A. Curtin, and Glen T. Cameron, "Diversity Advances Both Journalism, Business," *Newspaper Research Journal* (Spring 2001): 14.
23. Swanston, "The *Post* and Racial Diversity," 16.

Table 2 Editors' and staff members' morale by gender, 1982 and 2005

	Editors		Staff	
	1982	2005	1982	2005
Mean male morale	6.89	6.79	5.41	5.58
Mean female morale	7.06	6.49	5.07	5.33
Difference	−0.17	0.30	0.34	0.24

room, morale was sorted by gender in both 1982 and 2005 for editors and staff (see table 2).

In 1982, the mean morale perceived by female editors was greater than the mean morale seen by male editors, but in 2005 the male morale was greater. In both 1982 and 2005, the mean morale reported by male staff members was greater than that for female staff members. The more interesting finding is that in 2005 for both editors and staff members, the differences in the mean morale between males and females was smaller than it was in 1982, indicating that gender differences are not accounting for level of morale in the newsroom. But what, then, is the impact of diversity on news decisions?

News Decisions as a Reflection of Tolerance

In attempting to understand how newsrooms reflect community diversity, respondents were also asked two questions designed to measure attitude toward reflecting community diversity regarding religion and sexuality.

The first,

> Easter Sunday is approaching, and the editor plans the traditional one-page recognition of the holiday: A banner, 'He is risen.' Then a new publisher, who happens to be an agnostic, points out that the latest religious census shows the community to be six percent non-Christian.
>
> Should the editor:
> (1) Keep the Easter banner
> (2) Reduce the headline in deference to the non-Christians in the community

(3) Limit the paper's coverage to specific religious-oriented events scheduled for that day

(4) Avoid any mention of Easter

Editors showed a higher tolerance for religious diversity in 2005 than in 1982 (see table 3). In 1982, editors representing 50 percent of daily newspaper circulation responded that the banner should be kept. That figure dropped by 20 percentage points in 2005. These responses reflect the understanding that editors appear to be more sympathetic to religious diversity among the community in 2005 than they were in 1982.

Table 3 Editors' perspectives on Easter banner, 1982 and 2005[a]

	1982	2005
(1) **Keep the banner**	50%	29%
(2) **Reduce headline**	4	12
(3) **Cover events only**	46	57
(4) **Avoid mention**	1	1
Total	100%	100%

[a] Percents do not add to 100 due to rounding.

Notably, both surveys also included a question about attendance at religious services (see table 4). While respondents were free to answer never, less than once a year, about once or twice a year, several times a year, about once a month, two to three times a month, nearly every week or several times a week, for ease of analysis the responses were categorized into three categories: rarely, occasionally and frequently.[24]

Table 4 Editors' religious service attendance, 1982 and 2005

	1982	2005
Rarely	47%	35%
Occasionally	19	34
Frequently	34	31
Total	100%	100%

24. The following response choices were categorized as rarely: never, less than once a year, and about once or twice a year. Occasionally was defined as several

The survey data indicate that the frequency of religious service attendance for newspaper editors has increased since 1982.

With this information, we can use editors' religious service attendance as a measure against which to compare responses to the survey question about the Easter banner (see tables 5 and 6). Not surprisingly, in 1982 and 2005 editors who frequently attended religious services felt the strongest about keeping the Easter banner, while those editors representing daily newspaper circulation who rarely attended religious services felt strongest about covering events only. That is that editors who more frequently attend religious services are less tolerant of religious diversity in their communities, while editors representing daily newspaper circulation who attended religious services rarely are more tolerant of religious diversity in their communities.

The second question attempting to understand how newsrooms reflect community diversity questioned respondents about tolerance of sexual preferences. Although this question regarding the inclu-

Table 5 Editors' religious service attendance and perspectives on Easter banner, 2005

	Rarely	Occasionally	Frequently
(1) **Keep the banner**	28%	18%	41%
(2) **Reduce headline**	13	17	7
(3) **Cover events only**	58	64	50
(4) **Avoid mention**	1	1	2
Total	100%	100%	100%

Table 6 Editors' religious service attendance and perspectives on Easter banner, 1982

	Rarely	Occasionally	Frequently
(1) **Keep the banner**	39%	51%	62%
(2) **Reduce headline**	1	9	3
(3) **Cover events only**	59	40	33
(4) **Avoid mention**	1	0	2
Total	100%	100%	100%

times a year and about once a month. Frequently was defined as two to three times a month, nearly every week, every week, and several times a week.

sion of the gay angle in a story of a prominent citizen caught in a Key West hotel fire is addressed more fully in Chapter 6, editors' responses indicate increased sensitivity across time with respect to sexual diversity. In 2005, editors representing 30 percent of readers said they would publish the story in full, down from 41 percent in 1982.

Conclusion

Despite dedicated efforts by ASNE and other journalism organizations, newsroom employee diversity does not reflect the diversity seen in the American public. Although the gender divide has decreased since 1982, women still account for far less than half of all newsroom employees. In fact, the survey found that only 21 percent of daily newspaper circulation is served by female editors. Previous research has also indicated that racial diversity in newsrooms does not reflect the racial diversity in the population. Therefore, although newsrooms have a more diverse population in 2005 than they did in 1982, that diversity does not mirror the diversity in the U.S. population.

It is also vital for researchers to examine how newsrooms are reflecting community diversity. Although this survey did not dedicate much space toward questions about reflecting community diversity, several interesting findings did emerge. Most notably, religious service attendance by newsroom employees has increased since 1982. Overall, newsroom employees are showing an increased tolerance for religious diversity in their communities. However, those newsroom employees who reported frequent attendance at religious services, reflected less tolerance for respecting religious diversity among their readers. This finding held constant across 1982 and 2005.

The data found that in 2005, editors reflected a greater tolerance for sexual diversity than they did in 1982. However, the nature of the question must be further considered. In addition to having a gay component, the question also addressed an element of invasion of privacy. The citizen in question threatened to commit suicide if the article were published in full. So in addition to a greater respect for diversity, the data could also reflect a greater concern for the consequence to the subject of the story. Therefore, based on the nature of the question, the data cannot entirely be considered to reflect a greater tolerance for community diversity.

Based on these data points, the study can conclude that newsrooms are showing more concern for reflecting community diversity in 2005 than they were in 1982. However, reflecting community diversity has not reached an ideal state as intended in 1978 when ASNE established its goal to increase diversity.

A final area considered in the data was the relationship between employee gender and perceptions of newsroom morale. The study found that in 2005 for both editors and staff members, the differences in the mean morale between males and females was smaller than it was in 1982. This could be considered good news for the newspaper business. The gender of newsroom employees no longer appears to play a major role in affecting perceptions of newsroom morale.

It is evident that both newspaper organizations and newsrooms are devoting tremendous efforts and resources toward increasing newsroom diversity. The intention is that greater diversity among employees in newsrooms will lead to a greater reflection of community diversity within the pages of our newspapers. Despite this good intention and dedicated effort, this survey shows that diversity is not adequately reflected in newsrooms nor are newspapers doing an adequate job in reflecting the diversity within their communities.

CHAPTER 8

FINANCIAL CONFLICTS OF INTEREST

Rita F. Colistra

Good news for newspapers—they have not sold their souls for the almighty dollar just yet. Despite economic pressure from advertisers and stockholders, instances of financial conflicts of interest have decreased substantially since 1982. This is surprising given the large number of ethical scandals that have surfaced since 1982.

Early 2005 was a time that most journalism professionals would hope to soon forget. In the span of approximately one month, three syndicated conservative columnists, Armstrong Williams, Michael McManus and Maggie Gallagher, were revealed as receiving thousands of dollars to promote the Bush Administration's agendas.

Williams, who also hosts a cable television show, "The Right Side," received $240,000 to promote the No Child Left Behind Act through regular mentions on his broadcasts.[1] Gallagher was exposed for working under contract for the Department of Health and Human Services (HHS) while writing about the administration's Healthy Marriage Initiative.[2] She later apologized for not disclosing this information to her readers. One day later, McManus admitted in his online column, "Ethics and Religion," to praising the same marriage initiative and meeting with local organizers while receiving

---

1. Greg Toppo, "Education Dept. Paid Commentator to Promote Law," *USA Today* (Jan. 7, 2005), http://www.usatoday.com/news/washington/2005-01-06-williams-whitehouse_x.htm (accessed Jan. 9, 2005).

2. Howard Kurtz, "Bush Urges End to Contracts with Commentators," *Washington Post* (Jan. 27, 2005) http://www.washingtonpost.com/ac2/wp-dyn/A39872-2005Jan26, (accessed Jan. 27, 2005; Dave Astor, "Universal: Why We're Keeping Maggie Gallagher," *Editor & Publisher* (Jan. 26, 2005) http://www.editorandpublisher.com/eandp/departments/syndicates/article_display.jsp?vnu_content_id=1000777943 (accessed on Mar. 20, 2005).

a consulting fee from the HHS.[3] He, too, acknowledged that he should have disclosed the information. But, is disclosure enough? Or, should journalists simply refrain from any notion of a conflict—real or perceived?

A financial columnist for the *San Francisco Chronicle* suggested that he prefers the latter. In 1996, he told *American Journalism Review* (AJR), "If I do that [disclose], I'm putting my stamp of approval on it. Then I'm like an adviser.... If you are covering a [financial] beat, forget [owning stocks], no matter how good it sounds...."[4] Apparently he practices what he preaches. This same columnist considered buying stock in Toys 'R' Us to teach his children about investing but later disregarded the idea because of his position.

Since money is involved with financial conflicts of interest, it seems that the ethical line should be obvious: journalists should simply steer clear of any action where there is a financial reward involved. Ethics is not that clear-cut.

Take video news releases (VNRs) as an example. They have been the subject of major debates in the media world, especially in the United States. VNRs are public relations tools typically aimed at promoting a product, company, agenda, or person. These news releases are created to look like actual news stories and are distributed to television stations for broadcast. In some instances, stations run them without revealing that the video segments are produced by outside sponsors, agencies, or corporations. Thus, the public may not be able to distinguish between the VNR and a "real" news story put together by a station's news team. This was one of the factors in the Williams scandal. But, as the next example shows, even experienced journalists can get caught up in the sticky web of advertiser influences.

3. Dave Astor, "Columnist McManus Apologizes for Not Disclosing Federal Funding," *Editor & Publisher* (Feb. 3, 2005) http:// www.editorandpublisher.com/eandp/news/article_display.jsp?vnu_content_id=1000788577 (accessed on Feb. 3, 2005); Michael McManus, "Anatomy of an Ethical Lapse," http://marriage-savers.com/Columns/C1223.htm (accessed Feb. 3, 2005).

4. Kara Newman, "Walking a Tightrope," *American Journalism Review* (Oct. 1996): 36.

In May 2003, the *New York Times* uncovered a deal between two respected journalists and WJMK, a production company that creates VNRs.[5] Walter Cronkite and CNN's Aaron Brown both signed up to host a video series titled "American Medical Review," which ran on PBS. The problem was that the show was a VNR disguised as a newscast and was sponsored by corporations, such as drug manufacturers and health-care companies. The corporate sponsors, who paid around $15,000 to have their products featured in the VNRs, were trying to make their series more credible by hiring trusted journalists to host the show. And, they succeeded for several years with *60 Minutes'* Morley Safer as their host. Once the *New York Times* caught wind of the situation, both journalists called off the deal, and Safer sent letters to WJMK demanding that the company stop using videotapes of his appearances. [6]

This example shows that even renowned journalists and stations like PBS can get caught up in the financial influences on the media. In his book about public television, Hoynes assigns some of the blame to changes in the announcements of underwriting sponsors. Instead of mentioning the underwriters of a program, the messages have begun to sound more like actual advertisements as stations rely on outside sources for funding.[7]

Cronkite and Brown's case shows a more subtle instance of advertiser influences. But conflicts are not always so hidden; in fact, some are downright obvious. As one California news director put it, "The only thing remarkable about [the next case] is its blatancy."[8] He was speaking of an incident in which a FOX affiliate in Chattanooga was exposed for sending faxes that promised favorable coverage for a fee

---

5. Melody Peterson, "Walter Cronkite Backs away from Sponsored Video Deal," *New York Times* (May 9, 2003): 4C.

6. Deborah Potter, "Maybe It's Not So Obvious," *American Journalism Review* (June 2003): 64; Peterson, "Walter Cronkite."

7. William Hoynes, *Public Television for Sale: Media, the Market, and the Public Sphere* (Boulder, CO: Westview Press, 1994). See also Cindy Price, "Interfering Owners or Meddling Advertisers: How Network Television News Correspondents Feel about Ownership and Advertiser Influence on News Stories," *The Journal of Media Economics* (2003): 175–188.

8. Lou Prato, "Punishing the Ethically Challenged," *American Journalism Review* (Sept. 1999): 86.

of $15,000 to area businesses. According to *AJR*, an executive for the local owner blamed the incident on an overly aggressive sales team.[9]

With stories like these, it is no wonder that a 1998 Radio and Television News Directors Foundation (RTNDA) public survey showed that more than 80 percent of the respondents believed that advertisers have an "undue influence" over editorial content.[10] Whether it is a case of advertisers seeking out news organizations or news organizations seeking out advertisers, the driving force behind both situations is simple: money.

Shoemaker and Reese pointed out that radio and television stations are more susceptible to advertiser pressures than print media because they rely on these sources for revenue.[11] Despite this assertion, Price's study of ownership and advertising suggested that advertiser pressures on television may not be as extensive on the national level as one might think—at least to news correspondents. In 1999, she sent a survey asking about ownership and advertiser pressures to all correspondents working at the three network news stations, CNN, and PBS. Price found that only seven percent of the respondents mentioned even a rare influence.[12] It is important to note, however, that this figure may be low because only news correspondents were surveyed.

With all of the attention from the broadcast industry in recent years, it may have caused newspaper workers to talk about the possibility of advertiser influences within their *own* organizations. This was one of the issues put to editors in both the 1982 and 2005 ASNE surveys. In the surveys, the respondents were given a list of different kinds of ethical questions that newspapers sometimes face. For each one, they were asked to estimate how often cases of that type are discussed at their paper. Two examples were specifically aimed at financial conflicts of interest. The first deals with ethical discussions of pressures

---

9. Ibid.

10. Al Tompkins, "Balancing Business Pressure and Journalism Values," *Poynter Online* (Apr. 9, 2002) http://www.poynter.org/content/content_view.asp?id=3806 (accessed Nov. 25, 2005). See also, Prato, "Punishing the Ethically Challenged," 86.

11. Pamela J. Shoemaker and Stephen D. Reese, *Mediating the Message: Theories of Influences on Mass Media Content* (White Plains, NY: Longman, 1996).

12. Price, "Interfering Owners or Meddling Advertisers," 183.

from advertisers, such as blurbs, business-office musts, or pressure to keep things out of the paper or to get them in (see table 1).

Table 1 Editors' perception of discussion of pressures from advertisers, 1982 and 2005

	1982	2005
Less than once a year or never	21%	44%
Up to several times per year	53	41
At least monthly	26	15
	100%	100%

Since many ethical transgressions involving advertiser pressures have taken place since the 1982 survey, one might guess that these types of issues would be discussed more at newspapers. This, however, was not the case.

In 2005, editors representing 44 percent of U.S. daily circulation said advertiser pressures are never or rarely discussed at their papers. This translates into a 23 percentage-point increase from editors representing 21 percent in 1982. Why? Perhaps advertiser influences are less of a problem than in 1982. Still, it is likely that these influences occasionally surface. Newspaper workers would be wise to use the broadcast industry's transgressions as an opportunity to address such issues to prevent widespread occurrences in their own area.

Advertisers are not the only outside forces pressuring news organizations. Journalists are also pressured with economic temptations, such as gifts, theatre tickets, trips, or special discounts. But can a pair of cheap-seat tickets to a Jets game really influence the way a reporter covers a story? It might not matter. Actual influence and the perception of influence both straddle the same ethical line. What would happen if a reader found out that the local candidate for mayor gave you the tickets? Would the reader think you would be more willing to cover that candidate in a more positive light? The truth is, no one knows for sure, but my guess is yes. Although you might consider the gift as a friendly gesture, your readers may not see it that way. Oftentimes even the perception of a conflict is just as damaging to credibility as an actual conflict. Still, is accepting a few freebies that big a deal? The Society of Professional Journalists thinks so, and it is all laid out in its 1996 Code of Ethics. The section reads: "Journalists should be free of obligation to any interest other than the public's right to know.... Journalists should ... refuse gifts, favors, fees, free travel and special treatment."[13]

Despite the guidelines and timid climate of the media industry today, some journalists still believe that freebies are acceptable. In a survey of sports editors at southeast dailies, Hardin found that 43 percent thought that accepting freebies would not affect the objectivity of a sports reporter. Although a slight majority of the editors answered otherwise, the percentage suggests that accepting freebies remains a problem for the sports staff. This is not surprising given that 63 percent of the sports editors said their department discussed ethics only occasionally or rarely.[14]

Editors in both of our ASNE surveys were asked a similar question: how often were the following economic temptations of accepting trips, meals, favors, loans, gifts from sources or suppliers; or heavy socializing with sources discussed at their newspapers? Across time not much has changed (see table 2). The 2005 responses suggest that economic temptations are discussed much less than they were in 1982. In the 2005 survey, editors representing 43 percent of daily circulation said that this type of ethical situation is discussed less than once a year or never at their newspapers. This represents a small 15 percentage-point increase from the 1982 survey. If this practice, or non-practice, continues, it could mean that ethical lapses involving freebies are decreasing.

The two previous survey items concerned discussion of economic temptations, but what about actual occurrences of financial conflicts? To find out, the editors and staff in both ASNE surveys were asked the following:

> How often, to the best of your knowledge, does your
> paper publish editorial matter controlled by the business of-

---

13. Society of Professional Journalists Code of Ethics, http://www.spj.org/ethics_code.asp (accessed Sept. 21, 2005).

14. Marie Hardin, "Survey Finds Boosterism, Freebies Remain Problem for Newspaper Sports Departments," *Newspaper Research Journal* (Winter 2005): 66–72. Occasionally was defined as once or twice a month. Rarely was defined as less than once a month.

Table 2 Editors' perception of discussion of economic temptations from advertisers, 1982 and 2005

	1982	2005
Less than once a year or never	28%	43%
Up to several times per year	58	47
At least monthly	14	10
	100%	100%

fice on behalf of advertisers in the news columns (commonly known as "blurbs" or "business office musts")?

The responses are promising (see table 3). Both editors and staffers report that this type of conflict is happening much less often. Editors reporting that this type of action occurred less than once a year or never increased by 11 percentage points. The increase was even larger for staff members with 14 points, respectively. This finding suggests that although not much discussion of financial conflicts is taking place, editors and staffers report fewer instances of actual occurrences in 2005.

Table 3 Editors' and staff members' perceptions of business office influence on editorial content, 1982 and 2005

	Editors		Staff	
	1982	2005	1982	2005
Less than once a year or never	79%	90%	70%	84%
About once or twice a year or several times a year	14	7	18	10
About once a month or 2–3 times a month	4	2	5	4
Nearly every week or every week	2	2	5	2
Several times a week or daily	1	0	2	1
	100%	100%[a]	100%	100%[a]

[a] Percents do not add to 100 due to rounding.

Accepting gifts or favors from sources or suppliers is one thing, but what happens when journalists get paid to make speeches? This issue is the subject of another fierce ethical debate in the field. Ken Auletta addressed the issue in his book *Backstory: Inside the Business of News.* When asked why they should not be held to the same scrutiny as those in Congress when giving paid speeches, most of the interviewed journalists gave the same answers. First, many made the argument that journalists are private citizens, not elected officials like those in Congress. Others claimed that since they do not have control over public funds, they should not be held to the same standards as those in government.[15]

Next was the issue of outside income disclosure. Most of the journalists refused to divulge this information. *Times* columnist William Safire was an exception. He told Auletta that he gives around 15 speeches per year for $20,000 each. Several top journalists, however, give speeches, but either do not accept payment or donate the fees to charity. Still, ABC's Sam Donaldson sees nothing wrong with accepting payment for speeches. He reasoned, "[P]eople hire me because they think of me as a celebrity; they believe their members or the people in the audience will be impressed."[16] But, as Auletta pointed out, this type of perceived conflict of interest and entertainment-style journalism could lead to poor journalism and a further decline in credibility.

We asked editors and staff members to comment on a speaker's fee issue in both of our ASNE surveys:[17]

> An investigative reporter uses a computer to analyze criminal court records and writes a prize-winning series. A major computer manufacturer then offers to pay him $1,000 to speak at a seminar for reporters which it is sponsoring at a university.
> Which of the following best describes your view?
> (1) The reporter should be allowed to make the speech and accept the $1,000 from the computer manufacturer.

---

15. Ken Auletta, *Backstory: Inside the Business of News* (New York: Penguin Press, 2003): 185–199.

16. Ibid, 188.

17. The amount in 1982 question was $500, which was approximately equal to $1,000 in 2005.

(2) The reporter should be allowed to make the speech, but accept the $1,000 only if the honorarium is paid through the university.

(3) The reporter should be allowed to make the speech, but not to accept the honorarium.

(4) The reporter should not be allowed to make the speech.

Table 4 Editors' and staff members' perception of speaker fees, 1982 and 2005

	Editors		Staff	
	1982	**2005**	**1982**	**2005**
(1) **Collect the fee**	24%	11%	38%	12%
(2) **Launder it**	18	10	16	13
(3) **Speak for free**	51	65	41	60
(4) **Do not speak**	8	14	5	15
	100%	100%	100%	100%

The responses changed significantly since the 1982 survey (see table 4). Both editors and staff members are more concerned with financial conflicts of interest. Staff members saying the reporter should be allowed to accept the fee fell by 16 percentage points. This drop corresponds with significant increases in those that think the reporter should either speak for free or not at all. Changes were similar for editors, but not quite as dramatic. And the responses of staff members were more closely aligned with those of editors in 2005.

Overall, the ASNE surveys suggest that news workers representing total daily circulation in the U.S. are now more concerned with publicly observable conflicts of interest than they were in 2005—especially staffers. This may be due to the increased loss of credibility of newspapers due to ethical transgressions involving frontliners, such as the Stephen Glass and Jayson Blair scandals.

Another survey question asked editors and staff about perceived publisher behavior (see table 5).

How often does the publisher of your paper ask for special handling of an article about a company or organization which has some economic clout over your newspaper?

With the increasing pressures on publishers to make their newspapers profitable, an increase of this type of occurrence would seem likely. In fact, according to a *Quill* article, a recent survey of journalists conducted by four major media-workers unions found that 83 percent of the respondents cited "too much emphasis on the bottom line" as the media industry's most serious problem.[18] The same article referred to a separate survey that found 57 percent of journalists in local newsrooms and 66 percent in national newsrooms felt the "bottom-line pressure is seriously hurting the quality of news coverage."[19]

Table 5 Editors' and staff members' perceptions of publisher requests for special handling, 1982 and 2005

	Editors		Staff	
	1982	**2005**	**1982**	**2005**
Less than once a year or never	66%	79%	50%	72%
About once or twice a year or several times a year	30	19	43	24
About once a month or 2–3 times a month	2	1	6	3
Nearly every week or every week	1	0	1	1
	100%	100%	100%	100%

In the current research, both editors and staff members reported improvement. Editors who saw publisher conflict of interest occurring at least once a year represented 33 percent of daily circulation in 1982 but only 20 percent in 2005. The decline in staff cynicism was even steeper.

This is good news for both news people and journalism. Reporters and editors appear to be gaining autonomy which, in turn, should lead to better journalism and increased credibility in the public's eyes.

---

18. Michael Stoli and John McManus, "Downward Spiral," *Quill* (April 2005): 10.

19. Ibid.

While some newspapers may be pressured by companies that have economic clout over its operations, what happens when newspaper companies throw their money behind a cause? Such a question was asked in both the 1982 and 2005 ASNE surveys:

> Some newspaper companies in Florida donated money to a campaign to defeat a statewide referendum which, if passed, would have legalized gambling. Which of the following statements comes closest to your view on this action?
>
> (1) A newspaper that takes an editorial stand on an issue has a right, and possibly even a duty, to back up its belief with its money.
>
> (2) The contributions are justified if the referendum would have a detrimental effect on the business climate in which the newspaper operates.
>
> (3) The contributions should not have been made because they might lead readers to question the objectivity of the papers' news coverage.
>
> (4) No political contributions should ever be made by newspapers. The news and editorial columns make us powerful enough already, and adding money only indicates inappropriate hunger for more power.

Not much has changed with regard to this issue (see table 6). The only notable difference is among editors who think the business climate justifies the contribution. This moderate increase of nine percentage points may be due to emphasis on the bottom line, as mentioned earlier. Editors are likely more worried that if the business climate worsened as a result of the referendum, this, in turn, could also hurt their newspapers' profits.

Another major ethical dilemma facing news organizations and journalists is financial reporting. Covering Wall Street can be risky business for some reporters, as the economic temptations can be hard to resist. One well-known example occurred in the mid-nineties and involved a financial reporter, Dan Dorfman, who was accused of illegal trading. At the time, Dorfman worked as a commentator for CNBC and a columnist for *Money* magazine. An *AJR* article reported that he came under fire after critics accused him of market manipu-

Table 6 Editors' and staff members' perception of newspapers' political contributions, 1982 and 2005

	Editors		Staff	
	1982	**2005**	**1982**	**2005**
(1) **Right and duty**	11%	6%	6%	3%
(2) **Business justifies**	2	11	4	8
(3) **Hurts objectivity**	31	29	34	31
(4) **Should never contribute**	56	54	57	59
	100%	100%	100%[a]	100%[a]

[a] Percents do not add to 100 due to rounding.

lation as well as monetary deals with a Long Island stock promoter. He was later fired by *Money* magazine, but was retained by CNBC after an internal review process.[20]

Allegations like those in Dorfman's case and "busts" from outside the media industry, such as Enron and Tyco, have drawn even closer scrutiny to those involved with finance. But, what happens when you inadvertently "bust" yourself, albeit on a much smaller scale? That was the case in the example that follows:

> An investigative reporter does a thorough and praiseworthy expose of inequalities in tax assessment practices. In the course of investigating for the story, he looks at his own assessment records and finds that a value-enhancing addition to his property was never recorded, and as a result, his taxes are $600 less than they should be. He reports this fact in the first draft of his story, but, later, at the urging of his wife, takes it out.
> Should the editor:
> (1) Insist that he leave the information in, even though it will raise the reporter's taxes.
> (2) Talk to the wife and try to persuade her that the reporter's honesty at leaving it in will be rewarded, somehow.
> (3) Leave it to the reporter to decide, but appeal to his conscience.
> (4) Not interfere.

---

20. Newman, "Walking a Tightrope," 34.

No marked changes in opinion occurred from the 1982 to the 2005 ASNE surveys (see table 7). The majority of editors still believe he should leave it in, while the majority of staffers favor that option somewhat less. The second highest choice for both the editors and the staff members was letting the reporter decide himself. This illustrates the value of autonomy in decision-making in the newsroom. This has not changed much across the 23 years, nor is there any evidence that it is likely to change in the near future.

Table 7 Editors' and staff members' perception of full disclosure, 1982 and 2005

	Editors		Staff	
	1982	**2005**	**1982**	**2005**
(1) **Right and duty**	74%	79%	58%	55%
(2) **Business justifies**	4	1	2	5
(3) **Hurts objectivity**	17	13	29	27
(4) **Should never contribute**	5	7	11	13
	100%	100%	100%	100%

The major findings from the ASNE surveys regarding financial conflicts suggest that, although news workers representing total daily circulation are more concerned with the appearance of a conflict of interest, as evidenced by the responses on speaker fees, fewer ethical discussions regarding advertiser pressures are taking place in the newsroom. One reason may be that pressures from advertisers are likely to occur out of the public's direct attention. Instead, news people may be more focused on discussing only those pressures that are visible to their readers. This is not good because more ethical problems will probably transpire, and media credibility is likely to take a blow.

Another notable change in the 23-year period between the surveys was that most news people, especially staffers, responded that their publisher virtually never asked for special handling of a story concerning a company with financial clout over their newspaper. This is pleasing news for journalists, since it appears they are freer from management pressures. If we are lucky, the feeling of independence will spill over and help increase the quality of news reporting.

CHAPTER 9

NON-FINANCIAL
CONFLICTS OF INTEREST

Nathan Clendenin

Frequent discussion of issues involving non-financial conflicts of interest occurs in more newsrooms today than in 1982. This increase suggests an increase in transparency regarding non-financial conflicts of interest held by journalists.

As the *Dallas Morning News* discovered when it purchased part of the Dallas Mavericks basketball team, owning a news organization and a sports franchise in the same town has many tricky implications.[1] In 1999 the paper's owner, Belo Corp., paid $24 million for a small portion of the team which elicited city council member Donna Blumer's harsh rebuke, "Belo can no longer be an independent voice for the public." As was the case in this incident, many often jump to conclusions about conflicts of interest, especially when there is money involved in any capacity. In this case, Belo owned only 12.8 percent of the team, hardly a controlling portion. Nevertheless, the mere appearance of a conflict is enough to damage the paper's integrity. This example also reveals the common disconnect between those in a high position whose concern is the business and those "in the trenches" who try to remain unbiased and deal with conflicts of interest of a different sort. This chapter examines the variables from the 1982 and 2005 surveys dealing with non-financial conflicts of interest.

---

1. Kelly Heyboer, "Fair Game?," *American Journalism Review* (Oct. 1999): 47–50.

Background

Conflict of interest is a topic that is widely covered in various trade journals and media publications. Titles range from, "For many journalists, life is a conflict of interest," to "Publisher-public official: Real or imagined conflict of interest?"[2] The latter title belongs to a book that deals with the questions of conflicts of interest between politics and the media and focuses on larger figures like editors and publishers. The book mentions many former editors and publishers who ran and were elected to public office. One interesting article found in *Editor and Publisher* mentions a gay reporter who was transferred to the copy-editing desk for being involved in gay rights causes outside of work.[3] Upon protest from the gay community, the paper offered her the job back on the condition that she forgo participating in her political leadership roles, but she refused.

In a 2002 *Quill* article entitled "Is family a conflict?"[4] five different professionals gave their response to a scenario involving a political reporter whose wife was working for one of the local presidential candidates. Their responses varied greatly from absolute certainty to vagueness. Bill McCloskey, then director of media relations at BellSouth said, "I have never believed that accepting a job as a journalist requires one to become a political eunuch ... Before long a general assignment reporter would be rescued from covering half the news in town, especially a small town." Jerry Ceppos, then vice president/news at Knight Ridder, when asked if the reporter has a conflict of interest said, "Yes and yes. We're in the business of raising all sorts of questions about the appearance of impropriety where other people are involved. How can we ask for a pass when we're involved?" It seems that some take a flexible approach toward conflicts of interest while others make it a very black and white issue.

---

2. Don Sneed and Daniel Riffe, *The Publisher-Public Official: Real or Imagined Conflict of Interest?* (New York, NY: Praeger, 1992).

3. M.L. Stein, "Conflict of Interest or Anti-Gay Bias?" *Editor & Publisher* (Aug. 1994): 18.

4. Renita Coleman, Craig Freeman, and Judith Sylvester, "Is Family a Conflict?" *Quill* (July/Aug. 2002): 42–43.

An important question also appears in issues involving conflict of interest, and that is one of transparency. Do reporters consistently reveal their conflicts of interest? And do papers reveal to the public their political and financial ties openly enough? All the professionals taking part in the *Quill* article said yes. However, a study by the ASBE ethics committee published in 1986 said that even though editors at 87 percent of papers surveyed reported that employees had been dismissed or suspended for unethical behavior, no stories were published regarding the incidents.[5] With many papers being owned by larger companies who have ties with a variety of different entities, there is an apparent lack of transparency from the publisher's side of the paper as well. Is the degree of transparency changing?

J.D. Lasica argued in *Nieman Reports* that the transparency inherent in blogging has contributed to news organizations becoming more transparent.[6] She quoted Bill Kovach and Tom Rosenstiel from their book, *The Elements of Journalism*, "Journalists must invite their audience into the process by which they produce news." In examining the survey data we can get a glimpse of how editors and staff think about non-financial conflicts of interest.

Increasing Transparency

As reported in other chapters, both the 1982 and 2005 surveys asked editors about their perception of discussion of several important newsroom topics. Of interest here:

> Conflict of Interest: interest group activity by editors and publishers; service on boards and committees; campaign donations; stories involving financial interests of newspaper staff or management; spouse involvement.

---

5. Bruce Giles, "Newsroom Ethics: How Tough is Enforcement?" *Journal of Mass Media Ethics* (Fall/Winter 1986–87): 7–16.

6. J.D. Lasica, "Blogs and Journalism Need Each Other," *Neiman Reports* (Fall 2003): 70–74.

These issues are predominantly, if not purely, non-financial. Although more editors report such conflicts of interest being discussed at least monthly in 2005, the the number who discuss them less than once a year remained constant (see table 1).

Table 1 Discussion of non-financial conflict of interest in newsrooms, 1982 and 2005[a]

	1982	2005
Less than once a year or never	33%	32%
Up to several times per year	59	50
At least monthly	8	18
	100%	100%

[a] Editors only

Four variables in the 1982 and 2005 surveys work to pinpoint editor involvement outside the paper. If the respondent answered "bad idea" to the first question he or she was asked to answer the other three but otherwise skipped the rest of the series.[7] Each consecutive question decreases the role of a financial conflict moving toward non-financial conflicts of interest. The first,

> Do you think it's a good idea or a bad idea for a newspaper editor to serve on the board of another local company?

The second, which was only answered if respondent indicated "bad idea" to the first question,

> What if the company is non-profit, like a hospital or a symphony orchestra?

The third, which was only answered if respondent indicated "bad idea" to the first question,

> What if it was the board of a charitable enterprise like United Way or a local foundation?"

---

7. Possible responses: "bad idea," "good idea" or "no difference."

And the fourth, which was only answered if respondent indicated "bad idea" to the first question,

How about a church vestry or PTA board?

The majority of editors and staffers felt in 1982 and 2005 that serving of the board of a local company, a non-profit or a charitable enterprise is a "bad idea" (see table 2).

Table 2 Editors' and staff members' perception of editor's service as a bad idea, 1982 and 2005

	Editors		Staff	
	1982	2005	1982	2005
Local company	92%	95%	88%	83%
Non-profit company	78	80	74	74
Charitable enterprise	92	76	91	69
Church vestry or PTA	48	46	63	54

The only notable shift across time is among editors and staff members regarding charitable enterprises such as local foundations. Here, both groups appear to be relaxing their standards. Still perception of conflict of interest remains of concern.

In general in 2005, as the questions involved less perceived financial conflict of interest, the percentage of editors and staff members who said it was a "bad idea" decreased. This finding supports the "money is evil" theory, which says that editors and staff are more likely to think it is all right for editors to be involved in interests outside of the newsroom if they do not involve money.

Although the questions were designed to descend in order of less perceived conflict of interest, there was a surprising spike regarding involvement in charitable enterprises that dissipates in 2005. Perhaps charitable enterprises were not seen in as much of a positive light in 1982 as they are today.

It is interesting to note that by the final question the editors and staff representing half of daily newspaper circulation in the United States said it was a "bad idea," meaning the issue was split down the middle. This suggests that issues involving non-financial conflicts of interest are not easily decided in the newsroom.

Conclusion

As the newsroom continues to evolve to meet today's unique challenges, we should see a continued increase in discussion and awareness of ethical issues regarding non-financial conflicts of interest. This increase is imperative not only for staff who work in the trenches, whose goal is an objective method of reporting, but also extends to the business side of the paper. As more papers are bought and controlled by larger papers who have many financial and political ties, it is crucial that transparency and discussion about these potential conflicts of interest increase. Papers have already begun embracing the blog as a means of transparency, and this should also increase over time.

CHAPTER 10

NONE OF THIS IS MADE UP:
FABRICATION AND PLAGIARISM

Gabriel Dance

Despite plagiarism and fabrication having both been high-profile problems for newspapers recently, neither topic ranks high enough to warrant extended discussion in the newsroom. Instead, discussion seems to surround more mundane issues such as fairness and balance, taste in photos and invasion of privacy, according to the 2005 ASNE survey.

Background

In his influential essay "The Legend on the License," John Hersey clearly laid out the most serious tenet in journalism when he wrote, "The writer must not invent. The legend on the license must read: *NONE* OF THIS WAS MADE UP."[1] For the author, it was as clear a rule as could be, and one that had to be followed. Hersey wrote that the repercussions for failing to heed these words were that "Journalism is on a sickbed and is in a very bad way."[2] Hersey felt this problem had taken a serious turn for the worse when a few high-profile book authors, including Truman Capote and Tom Wolfe, began writing what was called "new journalism." The problem with this "new journalism" was that the authors combined both fact *and* fiction, but presented it as purely fact. Unfortunately, this led to more journalists trying the same thing, sometimes with disastrous results.

---

1. John Hersey, "The Legend of the License," *The Yale Review* (Oct. 1980): 2.
2. Ibid., 1.

In 1981, Janet Cooke wrote a truly moving series of stories for the *Washington Post* about an eight-year-old boy addicted to heroin. The pieces were regarded as brilliant journalism and Cooke won the Pulitzer Prize for her coverage. In the end, the story turned out to be fiction, and the *Washington Post* returned the prize and released the reporter.

In 1998, *The New Republic* discovered that an article written by Stephen Glass about a computer hacker who was hired to fix a company database was not true. After further investigation, it turned out Glass had fabricated nearly half of the stories he had written since coming to work for *The New Republic*.

In 2001, Jack Kelley, a veteran writer of 21 years for *USA Today*, wrote a fiercely gripping story detailing a suicide bombing in Jerusalem. As it turns out, Kelley actually didn't witness the bombing. Neither Kelley nor his editor kept their jobs.

And who could forget the *New York Times*' Jayson Blair? A promising young black writer, seemingly at the top of the journalism world, he was covering the biggest stories in the nation for one of the most renowned papers in the world. But in early 2004, after writing detailed descriptions concerning the family of then missing Pfc. Jessica Lynch, he was uncovered. Blair described the Lynch house as overlooking both tobacco fields as well as cattle pastures. It does not. After those articles, Blair did not work for the *New York Times* anymore. The *Times*' top two editors, Executive Editor Howell Raines and Managing Editor Gerald Boyd, both resigned shortly thereafter.

Hersey also clarified exactly why it was so terrible to commit journalism's original sin—or what Roy Peter Clark deemed the "unoriginal sin."[3] "The moment the reader suspects additions, the earth begins to skid underfoot, for the idea that there is no way of knowing what is real and what is not real is terrifying."[4] The idea of somebody who is expected to tell the truth inventing things that didn't really happen, and then passing them off as the truth, is tantamount to a doctor poisoning those he is supposed to heal.

---

3. Roy Peter Clark, "Unoriginal Sin," *Washington Journalism Review* (Mar. 1983).

4. Hersey, "The Legend of the License," 2.

The fact that the questions about plagiarism and fabrication that were included in the 2005 survey were not in the 1982 survey makes it difficult to explore trends regarding these issues over this time period. Meyer attributes the absence of the questions in the 1982 survey to the fact that the topics were not as prominent then as they are today. According to Meyer, "When the 1982 survey was designed, plagiarism and fabrication were so far below the radar that we saw no need to measure the frequency with which they were discussed in newsrooms." Even now these issues rarely reach the point where newsroom conversations have to be held about them.

Current State of Affairs

The subjects of plagiarism and falsification are tackled in the 2005 survey with two questions, similar in nature. The questions ask respondents how often plagiarism and fabrication are discussed at their newspapers.

As discussed, the 2005 ASNE survey contained several discussion-oriented questions in the same vein as the ones targeting plagiarism and fabrication. The focus of these questions included news methods, protecting sources, invasion of privacy, economic temptations, fairness and balance, suppression of news and several other categories. By comparing the responses for the questions we can determine the most talked about subjects and the least talked about subjects. Table 1 ranks them by the percent of daily newspaper circulation served by newspapers where each issue reaches the point where it causes conversation in the newsroom at least once a month. Of the 14 discussion questions with one being the most talked about and 14 being the least talked about, plagiarism ranks 11th and fabrication is last. Clearly, these are relatively rare problems.

For reasons unknown, editors at mid-size papers, those in the 50,000–250,000 range, were far less likely to report these two issues coming up for discussion than those at both smaller and larger papers. And female editors, by large multiples on the order of four to one, were more likely to report newsroom discussion of plagiarism or fabrication.

Table 1 Editors' perceptions of most commonly discussed newsroom issues, 2005

Newsroom Issue	Percentage discussion about once a month or more often
Fairness and balance	77%
Photos	44
Protecting sources	32
Invasion of privacy	28
Conflict of interest	18
Government secrecy	16
Advertiser pressure	15
Economic temptations	10
News methods	9
Plagiarism	4
Civil disorder	2
Non-news tasks	2
Suppression of news	2
Fabrication	2

Neither the youngest nor the oldest editors were as aware of conversations about these issues as those in the middle. Most of the reporting of newsroom conversations about plagiarism or fabrication came from editors with 11 to 30 years of newspaper experience.

Conclusion

The 2005 survey does not include information regarding whether or not fabrication or plagiarism has occurred at the surveyed newspapers, only whether or not the issues were discussed. It can be assumed that subjects are discussed in a newsroom most often when they occur or are suspected in that newsroom. However, with topics such as fabrication and plagiarism, it seems natural that they are discussed whenever they have a significant impact on the industry, as was true with Jayson Blair and many of the previous high-profile examples.

Assuming that is the case, the data gathered from the survey is surprising. With so many infamous scandals in the recent past it is a wonder that plagiarism is discussed less frequently than 10 other newsroom topics, and fabrication less frequently than 13 other topics.

On the other hand, these data offer some reassurance that the *Times* and *USA Today* fabrication cases were anomalies and not typical of the industry as a whole.

CHAPTER 11

PROTECTING SOURCES

Anne J. Tate

A recent rash of scandals involving anonymous sources—from the Jayson Blair fabrications at the *New York Times* to the *Newsweek* Koran-flushing story retraction—has made editors apprehensive about letting their reporters grant confidentiality to sources. Yet, the 2005 study shows that most papers still use anonymous sources and that newsroom discussions of the issue of granting confidentiality are no more frequent than they were 23 years ago.

On the other side of the coin, the high-profile CIA leak case that sent the *New York Times'* reporter Judith Miller to jail and led to *Time* magazine's Matthew Cooper handing his notes over to federal prosecutors has stirred debate about the ability of journalists to protect confidential sources. Yet, neither perceived pressure from the public nor hard economic times has weakened newspaper editors' resolve to hew to pledges of confidentiality.

This chapter will attempt to assess newsroom attitudes toward these issues by examining the results of the 2005 ASNE survey and—when possible—comparing them to those from the 1982 survey. Has the climate changed since 1982 regarding confidentiality and government secrecy? How often do editors talk about these issues? Do newspapers have policies regarding confidentiality? Do they use anonymous sources? And how vigorously do newspapers protect sources and how often do they publish grand jury leaks?

Background

Anonymous Sources

Recently, many newspapers have rewritten policies on anonymous sources, perhaps trying to stem the rampant use of anonymous sources that might make them appear untrustworthy to an increasingly skeptical public. It appears this concern has had an effect. A 2005 State of the Media Report shows newspapers print significantly fewer stories citing anonymous sources than they did one year ago.[1]

Although the public seems to be consistently losing faith in the news media, the majority of Americans believe reporters should be able to use anonymous sources. A 2004 poll by the First Amendment Center and the American Journalism Review found that 70 percent of Americans believe journalists should be allowed to keep sources confidential. According to the same poll, 77 percent believe in the role of the press as a watchdog in a democratic society.[2] In addition, a study sponsored by Associated Press Managing Editors showed that more than half—53 percent—of the 1,611 readers they surveyed said the use of anonymous sources did not negatively affect their trust of a news story.[3] So, while the public remains supportive of the practice, concerns about granting confidentiality within journalism circles persist.

According to most articles on anonymous sources, the pervasive complaint among editors is that confidentiality is offered too readily and too often by reporters. While there is little to no quantitative data to prove them right or wrong, a non-scientific telephone survey of 419 media outlets, sponsored by the Associated Press Managing Editors (APME), revealed that three-quarters of news organizations permit their reporters to use anonymous sources. The remaining one in four, however, claimed they have banned the practice entirely.[4] "We might as well be writing fiction if we can't give our readers a source," said Ana Walker, editor of the *Longview (Texas) News-Journal*, which has not used an anonymous source in the last 10 years.[5]

---

1. Tom Rosentstiel, "A Downward Trend in Use of Anonymous Sources," *Neiman Reports* (Summer 2005): 38.

2. Paul McMasters, "Low Marks," *American Journalism Review* (Aug./Sept. 2004): 72.

3. Ryan Pitts, "Readers Describe Use of Anonymous Sources as 'Double-Edged Sword,'" *Spokane Spokesman-Review* (June 17, 2005).

4. Ibid.

5. Joe Strupp, "Losing Confidence," *Editor & Publisher* (July 2005): 34.

From a policy-making standpoint, larger papers are becoming more cautious about the practice. *USA Today*, which has traditionally been conservative about granting anonymity, recently tightened its restrictions, now requiring a reporter to answer a battery of questions successfully before going to print with an unnamed source.[6] The *New York Times* instituted a policy of editor notification for confidentiality in February 2004, after the Jayson Blair scandal broke. The *Washington Post* followed suit.[7]

It appears this hesitation has resulted in a drop in the use of anonymous sources. The Project for Excellence in Journalism examined 16 newspapers of varying sizes and found that a mere seven percent of all stories contained an unnamed source—that's down from 29 percent a year ago. The same study showed that papers with larger circulation are more likely to use anonymous sources.[8]

While most journalists agree that confidentiality is used too frequently, they argue it would be impossible to report in highly secretive environments—such as Washington—without the option of source protection. There's actually an anecdote that supports this contention. Thirty years ago and right before the famous Watergate case, Ben Bradlee, then executive editor of the *Washington Post*, banned the use of anonymous sources at his paper. Bradlee was tired of being played by Nixon-era politicians, so he decreed his staff could no longer use unnamed sources. The experiment lasted just two days. The *Post* was being scooped left and right, making it clear that reporting on the federal government requires some degree of source protection.

While political reporters require some latitude when it comes to anonymous sources, many argue that this protection is still offered too readily. Mike McCurry, who served as one of President Bill Clinton's press secretaries, said reporters often proposed confidentiality before he even had a chance to request it. "I've had probably thousands of conversations with reporters in 25 years as a press secretary,

---

6. Roundtable discussion with Geneva Overholser, "Reporting in an Era of Heightened Concern about Anonymous Sources." *Neiman Reports* (Summer 2005): 39–41.

7. Strupp, "Losing Confidence ," 34.

8. Rosentstiel, "A Downward Trend," 39.

and I'd say 80 percent of the time I am offered anonymity and background rather than asking for it," McCurry said.[9]

Reporter's Privilege

The debate about granting confidentiality brings up the tangential issue of protecting anonymous sources—a topic that has received its own share of media attention lately. The CIA leak case, in which a high-ranking White House official leaked the identity of covert CIA agent Valerie Plame Wilson—ostensibly in retribution for her husband's criticism of the Bush administration—has shined a spotlight on federal shield laws or lack thereof. Judith Miller of the *New York Times* and Matthew Cooper of *Time* magazine were cited for contempt of court for refusing to reveal their confidential sources to a grand jury in the prosecution of this case. Cooper eventually gave up his notes, at the behest of his editor, Norman Pearlstein. Miller, on the other hand, was sent to jail. The result has been a cascade of articles about reporter's privilege and the need for a federal shield law. As of spring 2005, there were about 30 journalist subpoenas pending in federal courts, according to the Reporters Committee for Freedom of the Press.[10]

The Plame case, among others, makes it clear that reporter's privilege in the United States is eroding. The Reporters Committee points out that the number of journalists currently facing federal subpoenas "far exceeds the reporters' privilege crisis of the Nixon years."[11] At the same time, more foreign countries are passing laws protecting reporters—in Sweden, for example, journalists are prevented by law from revealing their confidential sources.[12] Although 31 states have some form of a shield law and there are bills before both houses of Congress proposing protections at the federal level, the amount of privilege journalists can expect remains uncertain. To make matters

---

9. Roundtable discussion with Geneva Overholser, "Offering Anonymity Too Easily to Sources." *Nieman Reports* (Summer 2005): 42–44.

10. Lucy Dalglish, "Protecting Reporters Who Protect Sources." *Neiman Reports* (Summer 2005): 32.

11. Ibid.

12. Ibid.

murkier, in the 1972 landmark Supreme Court case dealing with confidentiality, Branzburg v. Hayes, the majority ruled that reporters are not exempt from testifying before a federal grand jury. Also, *Branzburg* was such a divided decision—4–1–4—that it provides little guidance for rulings today.

No doubt, the use of anonymous sources has always sparked debate among editors and reporters. And the American media has had similar crises of faith in the past—look no further than the Janet Cooke incident at the *Washington Post* in 1981. But recent events have roiled these waters and renewed journalists' paranoia about credibility and privilege.

A Change

The 1982 and 2005 surveys share four of the same questions about confidentiality, allowing for analysis of these issues across time. Other questions regarding policy-making and use of anonymous sources are new to the 2005 version.

Discussion Levels

The first two questions the surveys have in common assess how often source protection and government secrecy (grand jury leaks and national security problems, including military secrets and diplomatic leaks) are discussed in the newsroom. With all the controversy and heightened media awareness about anonymous sources and the famous secrecy of the Bush administration, we might imagine these are big concerns among editors. Surprisingly, though, the data show these issues are usually only occasionally talked about, and the frequency of discussion about these topics has even decreased during the past 23 years (see tables 1 and 2). In 2005, discussion of the sourcing issue occurred at least once a year at newspapers representing 82 percent of circulation, a 12 percentage-point drop from 1982 when that percentage was 94.

Discussion of government secrecy has followed the same trend. In 2005, editors representing 58 percent of newspaper circulation said this topic was discussed at least yearly as compared to 85 percent in 1982.

Table 1 Editors' perception of discussion of protecting sources, 1982 and 2005

	1982	2005
Less than once a year or never	6%	18%
Up to several times per year	59	50
At least monthly	35	32
	100%	100%

Table 2 Editors' perception of discussion of government secrecy, 1982 and 2005

	1982	2005
Less than once a year or never	15%	42%
Up to several times per year	67	42
At least monthly	18	16
	100%	100%

To put these numbers in perspective, however, it's important to consider that the relative importance of these issues in the newsroom has remained pretty much the same, with protection of sources being the fourth most discussed topic both in 1982 and 2005.

Policy and Use

One conceivable explanation of the apparent discrepancy between the great attention these seemingly hot topics receive in the media and the relatively scant interest they get in the newsroom is that many papers might have policies that remove the need for debate. Articles in trade journals certainly indicate that more papers are developing or rethinking regulations on anonymous sources. In fact, newspapers representing 77 percent of circulation have a policy on anonymous sources, and 56 percent of those recently revamped their policy. Because the 1982 survey did not ask the same questions, we cannot measure whether this is a new phenomenon. What's interesting, though, is that having a source policy has at least a small effect of stimulating newsroom discussion about anonymous sources.

Table 3 Frequency of discussion of anonymous sources and presence of a source policy, 2005[a]

	Source policy	No source policy
Less than once a year or never	16%	23%
Up to several times per year	52	45
At least monthly	32	32
	100%	100%

[a] As perceived by editors

Editors representing 98 percent of circulation will allow their reporters to use anonymous sources in some way, but there is great variance in the degrees of restriction. The 2005 survey asked, "In general, whether or not you have a written policy, which of the following comes closest to your view on the use of unnamed sources?" The responses of editors are shown in Table 4—with papers representing 81 percent of circulation permitting source confidentiality when it's the only way to get a story. And editors representing 88 percent of circulation say they require reporters to consult editors before they use unnamed sources. This finding jibes with the trend of policy-making we see in agenda-setting papers like *USA Today*, the *New York Times* and the *Washington Post*.

Table 4 Editors' views on anonymous sources, 2005

Anonymous sources ...	Editors 2005
Should never be used in any way.	2%
Can be used only to guide reporters to information that is on the record and can be verified.	12
Can be used whenever there is a clear and overriding public interest in information that cannot be obtained any other way.	81
Can be used at the reporter's discretion, but reporters should be cautioned not to overdo it.	5
Are often vital to the free flow of information and should be encouraged.	0
Total	100%

According to the data, circulation size affects policy and use of anonymous sources (see table 5). Medium and large papers are more likely to have a policy on anonymous sources. About 30 percentage points separate the smallest newspapers from those with medium to large circulations.

Table 5 Circulation and presence of a source policy, 2005

| | | *Circulation* | |
	Small (circ. 50,000 or less)	**Medium** (circ. 50,001– 250,000)	**Large** (circ. 250,001 or more)
Have policy	54%	88%	85%
No Policy	46	12	15
Total	100%	100%	100%

For respondents who indicated their newspaper had a written source policy, a follow-up question targeted how current the policy was (see table 6). Here a more fluid trend is apparent. The likelihood of the source policy being redone increased with the circulation of the newspaper, from editors representing 44 percent of readership at small papers, to 55 percent at medium papers and 65 percent at large papers.

Table 6 Circulation and recent revision of a source policy of those newspapers with a formal policy, 2005

| | | *Circulation* | |
	Small (circ. 50,000 or less)	**Medium** (circ. 50,001– 250,000)	**Large** (circ. 250,001 or more)
Recently redone	44%	55%	65%
Not recently redone	56	45	35
Total	100%	100%	100%

In keeping with this trend in the data, papers with smaller circulation also use anonymous sources less often than those with larger circulations.

Reporter's Privilege

Even in the wake of the dramatic CIA leak case, newspapers appear to believe more strongly in reporter's privilege. The data show that newspapers are more adamant about never violating pledges of confidentiality than they were in 1982 (see table 7). In the most recent survey, editors at newspapers representing 28 percent of circulation said they believe these types of pledges should always be kept versus only 20 percent in 1982.

Table 7 Editors' perception of keeping pledges of confidentiality, 1982 and 2005

	1982	2005
Should always be kept	20%	28%
Break in unusual circumstances	71	67
Judge by potential harm	9	5
Pledges not serious	0	0
	100%	100%

As might be predicted, papers with larger circulation—for the most part—are more likely to keep pledges of confidentiality.

Government Secrecy

The press appears to be serious about its role as a government watchdog. As we have already determined, papers are getting fiercer in their defense of reporter's privilege. In addition, editors in the 2005 survey are more willing to publish grand jury leaks "whenever they are news" now than they were 23 years ago, by a margin of 17 percentage points; editors representing 36 percent of newspaper circulation in 2005 will publish leaks whenever they are newsworthy versus editors representing 19 percent of newspaper circulation in 1982.

For both years, papers with larger circulations generally had looser criteria for publishing leaks.

Conclusion

These two surveys give us some interesting data to chew on, but follow-up questions would be needed to flesh out the meaning behind the responses. For instance, we learned that papers with larger circulations—and usually public ones—are more likely to use anonymous sources, keep pledges of confidentiality and publish grand jury leaks. Why is this? We might hypothesize that smaller papers are less likely to generate original coverage of Washington, obviating much of the need for anonymous sources. It would be useful in further research to canvass the kinds of stories that use unnamed sources most frequently.

Also, the absence of questions about use of anonymous sources and policies on the subject on the 1982 survey prevent comparison over time. We could, however, do some deep historical research and find out the number of papers that had policies on anonymous sources in 1982. This data would be helpful in tracing the evolution of policy-making on confidentiality over the years.

The most curious result of this data illustrates a startling discrepancy between how often confidentiality and government secrecy are discussed in the media and how often they are discussed on the job. Why is there such low discussion in newsrooms of such seemingly hot journalistic topics? The idea that policy precludes the need to talk about anonymous sources is not supported by the data. Is it such an accepted practice, it's not really fodder for debate? Is it because reporters spend so little time at their desks, chatting with their peers? Is it because most reporters—especially neophytes—are not writing the kind of stories that require the protective measure of anonymity? More questions, or perhaps more specific responses, on the subject would be needed to determine why these issues are not vigorously debated in the newsroom.

CHAPTER 12

DECLINING SUPPORT FOR
NEWS COUNCILS

Ryan Campbell

News councils have been controversial in the United States, where journalists tend to resist any suggestion of public oversight. But in a few places where they have been tried, news councils have proven quite effective without bringing an end to freedom of the press. Despite this history, this research reveals that support for news councils has decreased since 1982 among newspaper editors and staff members.

News councils operate as independent bodies to resolve complaints by individuals or companies against a news organization, such as accusations of unfair or biased coverage. There are, however, some important distinctions about news councils. First, they answer to no one, priding themselves on an independence that permits their neutrality. Second, they have no power to levy punishment against the press but are able to tarnish a newspaper's most valuable commodity—its credibility. With that, the primary caveat for complaints submitted to news councils is that all parties must agree not to sue once the case has been heard.

Despite these advantages, only three states—Minnesota, Washington and Hawaii—currently have functioning news councils. The National News Council has been defunct since 1984. This evidence suggests that support for news councils is weakening. To address this specifically, one question in the 1982 and 2005 survey focused on news councils:

Do you agree or disagree?
A state news council, modeled after the National News Council, would be a good idea?

The change over time reveals a stark difference between editors' and staff members' support of news councils (see table 1).

Table 1 Editors' and staff members' perceptions of news councils as a good idea, 1982 and 2005

	Editors		Staff	
	1982	**2005**	**1982**	**2005**
Agree	28%	20%	45%	38%
Disagree	70	69	48	30
Don't know[a]	2	11	7	31
Total	100%	100%	100%	100%[b]

[a] Only "agree" and "disagree" were possible responses on the questionnaire. The "don't know" category was created by aggregating the missing responses.
[b] Percent adds to less than 100 because of rounding.

The data confirm that news councils have never been popular among editors. In 2005, editors representing 69 percent of newspaper readers thought news councils were a bad idea, while staff representing only 30 percent opposed state news councils. Both figures, however, represent a decline in support since 1982.

If we assume that the non-responses are due to lack of knowledge about news councils, these time-series data reveal a clear increase among both groups in ignorance about news councils—a 9 percentage point jump among editors and a shocking 24 percentage point jump among staff members. This relatively high rate of blank answers, indicated by "don't know," could indicate that fewer journalists were familiar enough with news councils to be comfortable answering a question that dealt with them. Is this striking disparity between editors and staff members actually an indication of an age difference between the groups? That is, in 2005, young reporters are not likely well versed regarding the function of news councils. In fact, many may not be familiar with news councils at all. We can address this specifically by examining the age of respondents and their answer to the question at hand (see table 2).

Evidenced by the percentage of "don't know" responses, younger respondents are more ignorant about news council than older respondents. It appears that this may also be coupled with a naiveté, as

Table 2 Perceptions of news councils as a good idea by age, 2005

	35 years old and younger	36 to 39 years old	50 years old and older
Agree	40%	30%	25%
Disagree	31	46	62
Don't Know[a]	30	23	14
Total	100%[b]	100%[b]	100%[b]

[a] Only "agree" and "disagree" were possible responses on the questionnaire. The "don't know" category was created by aggregating the missing responses.
[b] Percent adds to less than 100 because of rounding.

young respondents are also significantly more likely to support state news councils. Despite this slight up note, the waning support for news councils is clear.

However, had the question used the Minnesota News Council as its model news council rather than the failed National News Council, which ran from 1973 to 1984, support might have been even higher. Gary Gilson, executive director of the Minnesota News Council said that many people who object to news councils either don't know what they are or they associate them with the National News Council: "There is a great deal of emotional baggage associated with the National News Council."[1]

In an interview with Fred Brown of *Quill*, freelance writer Peter Sussman said, "I am suspicious of any group, however respected and respectable, serving a judicial or quasi-judicial role, passing judgments on journalistic practices."[2] He continued, "It can all too easily become a kind of 'shadow government' of journalism, a very dangerous notion. People are looking for solid 'official conclusions' in an uncertain world, and news councils appear to provide them, whether that is what they intend or not—and whether such clear conclusions are possible or not."[3]

Notably however, pockets of support for news councils have been growing since the Knight Foundation offered two $75,000 start-up

---

1. Gary Gilson, personal phone conversation, Oct. 2005.
2. Fred Brown, "Push for More News Councils Sparks Debate, Controversy," *Quill* (Sept. 2005): 32.
3. Ibid.

grants to anyone who can establish a viable state news council. The national competition is being organized by the Minnesota and Washington councils and applicants "must demonstrate the ability to raise additional funds, including a significant portion from media organizations, to support operations for at least three years." The Knight Foundation grant, "really stirred up the troops," said Gilson.[4]

To better understand news councils, and the controversy surrounding them, we should take a look back at their origins in the heyday of newspapers. With funds from legendary media mogul Henry Luce, a group of professionals and scholars, headed by University of Chicago chancellor Robert M. Hutchins, set out to assess the state of press freedom in the U.S. The Hutchins Commission, as it was called, published its findings in 1947 report, "A Free and Responsible Press." The report exposed fissures among press media organizations and divided journalists between two camps: those who cringe at the hint of restraint, and those who uphold the social responsibility aspect of journalism. Since the report was disseminated well before television had gained its footing, one can only imagine how that gap has widened in the decades since the commission published its groundbreaking work.

The report found three basic problems afflicting the American press. The commission said that fewer people were gaining more influence over a larger audience. Secondly, it said that the press was not adequately meeting its social obligations. Finally, and most telling for our purposes, the commission determined that a continuation of the questionable tactics being used to gather and report the news would eventually lead to a public outcry and government regulation.

The press, the commission ruled, had failed to provide "a service adequate to the needs of society." The commission offered five recommendations to improve the state of the press and stave off regulation. To bring about these policies and ensure that the media continue to follow them, the commission proposed "the establishment of a new and independent agency to appraise and report annually upon the performance of the press." This agency needed to be inde-

---

4. Gilson, personal phone conversation.

pendent from both the government and the press, and the group must be funded by private donations alone.

The commission's report would prove a harbinger of many things, but perhaps most significantly it was the first to call for an official, independent press oversight body. Future news councils would go on to use some of the report's mandates as base for their official mission statements. According to National News Council Director Richard P. Cunningham, the report "set out for the first time what came to be called the social responsibility theory of the press, the idea that in return for its constitutional guarantee of freedom—a guarantee accorded to no other business —the press owed a debt to the community."[5]

The report was not well received by newspaper publishers and editors who criticized the commission for not containing any professional journalists. Its frequent warnings of impending government regulation and public outrage did not endear the commission to most media organizations. According to Cunningham, the pessimistic report was overshadowed by positive post World War II vibes and promptly ignored.

As America's fortunes began to change with the civil rights movement, emerging drug culture and Vietnam War, the strain on the free press began to grow. The formerly rock-solid influence of newspapers was increasingly giving way to television news. Richard Nixon and his cohorts lashed out at journalists critical of his administration. In his book, "The Short Life of the National News Council," Patrick Brogan credited the attacks on press freedom by Nixon and his staffers as the impetus for the creation of an independent body to review the state of journalism, the National News Council.

But the news council failed to garner support from several top news organizations, most notably the *New York Times*. *Times* publisher, Arthur Ochs Sulzberger, along with *Washington Post* Editor Ben Bradlee thought the council dangerous to the freedom of the press and tried to deep-six the venture at every turn.

---

5. Richard P. Cunningham, "Why Did One News Council Fail and the Other Succeed?" Organization of News Ombudsmen, http://www.newsombudsmen.org/ cunning3.html (accessed Jan. 10, 2006).

Shortly before his death, Cunningham wrote about his experience with the National News Council. "It is my opinion that the task force made a major mistake by establishing a national council in the face of such opposition. It would have been better to seek out progressive editors and publishers and to support the fund in the formation of state or regional councils. Then both journalists and the public would have had a chance to become accustomed to the work of news councils—as the journalists and the public of Minnesota have."[6] The main problem with the National News Council, however, was that it took the wrong approach in dealing with cases. It actively went after cases rather than wait for complaints to be brought before its board. It was also limited by its mandate to only handle complaints against national news organizations.

The initial foundation funding had run out by the early 1980s and in response the Council ended its ban on taking donations from news organizations. It would prove too little, too late. The Council failed to acquire influence and national-news providers disregarded its complaints. Journalist Emerson Stone said, "The National News Council largely died because the *New York Times* made them seem like they were going after the freedom of the press."[7]

By contrast, the Minnesota News Council is widely considered to be a success. It was established in response to calls by the Minnesota Newspaper Association in the late 1960s for an independent body. Public trust in the news media was declining, they thought, and the state needed some way to resolve complaints and restore trust in the media. Using the British Press Council as a model, they founded a news council of their own.

With a budget of $225,000, the Minnesota News Council is comprised of 24 volunteer members—half from the media; half from disciplines as varying as law and academe. Major corporations including 3M and General Mills contribute 40 percent of needed funding, 30 percent comes from foundations, 10 percent comes from the news organizations themselves and 20 percent comes from private indi-

---

6. Ibid.
7. Emerson Stone, personal phone conversation, Nov. 2005.

viduals. The Council deals with 385 newspapers, including 25 dailies and 15 television stations in Minnesota.

Gina Lubrano, Executive Secretary of the Organization of News Ombudsmen, doubts the feasibility of news councils for anything other than large corporate media operating in a big city. "Newspapers should have someone who can handle local complaints so that they don't have to go to a news council," she said.

Another common worry among news organizations is that council rulings will eventually be acquired by lawyers and used as precedent in court cases. Stanford University professor Ted Glasser said this isn't likely and overlooks the real benefit of news councils. "I don't know of any instances where news council decisions have been entered into evidence in, say, a libel trial, but I am familiar with some very compelling evidence that mechanisms like news councils head off litigation by providing a much-needed safety valve for people who feel wronged by the press."

Despite the success of the Minnesota News Council, editors and staff members demonstrate declining support for state news councils. Therefore if news councils are to gain a toehold, they will have to turn a very big ship—journalists' opinions—in order to gain the support of the major media outlets in their respective states.

PLEASE HELP US UNDERSTAND
TODAY'S ETHICAL ISSUES!

Current Practices

1. Does your paper have a regular ombudsman column?

	Editors	
Response	**1982**	**2005**
Yes	15	20
No	85	80

2. (IF YES TO Q. 1) Is the ombudsman chosen by the editor or by someone independent of the editor?

	Editors	
Response	**1982**	**2005**
Chosen by editor	65	86
Chosen by someone else	36	14

3. Does the editor read the ombudsman's copy before it is published?

	Editors	
Response	**1982**	**2005**
Yes	37	53
No	63	47

4. (IF YES TO Q. 3) Does the editor read the ombudsman's copy for information or to approve it?

	Editors	
Response	**1982**	**2005**
Information	89	78
Approve it	11	22

5. Does your paper have a written policy on the use of anonymous sources?

Response	Editors 2005
Yes	77
No	23

6. (IF YES TO Q. 5) Has the policy been revised or rewritten in the past two years?

Response	Editors 2005
Yes	57
No	44

7. In general, whether or not you have a written policy, which of the following comes closest to your view on the use of unnamed sources.

1. Anonymous sources should never be used in any way.
2. Anonymous sources should be used only to guide reporters to information that is on the record and can be verified.
3. Anonymous sources can be used whenever there is a clear and overriding public interest in information that cannot be obtained in any other way.
4. Anonymous sources can be used at the reporter's discretion, but reporters should be cautioned not to overdo it.
5. Anonymous sourcing is often vital to the free flow of information and should be encouraged.

Response	Editors 2005
Statement 1	2
Statement 2	12
Statement 3	81
Statement 4	5
Statement 5	0

8. Does your newspaper require reporters to consult with editors in *every* case of anonymous sourcing?

Response	Editors 2005
Yes	88
No	12

9. Here is a list of different ways that newspapers handle corrections and amplifications. Please tell me which one comes closest to your paper's policy.

1. Corrections appear under a standing head, anchored to a specific place in the paper.
2. Corrections appear under a standing head which floats as needed.
3. Corrections are run as needed, without a standing head or a particular location in the paper.
4 Corrections are normally not made. The most we'll do is run another version of the story to get a correct version in the paper, but without acknowledging that it is a correction.
5. No correction of any kind is made.

| | Editors | |
Response	1982	2005
Statement 1	55	93
Statement 2	21	6
Statement 3	24	1
Statement 4	0	0
Statement 5	0	0

10. Which statement best describes your newspaper's Web site?

1. Closely integrated with the newsroom and uses the same content.
2. Closely integrated with the newsroom but generates some original content.
3. Only loosely connected to the newsroom.
4. Both physically and organizationally separate from the newsroom.
5. My newspaper does not have a Web site.

| | Editors |
Response	2005
Statement 1	30
Statement 2	58
Statement 3	4
Statement 4	9
Statement 5	0

11. Do you or any other journalist representing your newspaper interact with readers on a regular basis through a Web log or blog?

Response	Editors 2005
Yes	40
No, and none planned	26
No, but being considered	35

12. (IF YES TO Q. 11) Which is your most common way of correcting factual errors on your Web logs:

1. Correct the original copy without acknowledging that an error occurred.
2. Leave the error, but insert a correction adjacent to or just after it appears.
3. Leave the error but insert a correction at the bottom of the story.
4. No fixed policy – we are still experimenting with corrections.

Response	Editors 2005
Statement 1	24
Statement 2	11
Statement 3	6
Statement 4	59

Ethical Issues

Here is a list of different kinds of ethical questions that newspapers sometimes face. For each one, please estimate how often cases of that type are discussed at your paper.

13. News gathering methods: using false identity; stolen documents; concealed recording; eavesdropping.

Response	Editors 1982	2005
Never	28	36
Less than once a year	19	21
About once or twice a year	28	19

Several times a year	18	16
About once a month	4	5
Two or three times a month	2	3
Nearly every week	2	0
Several times a week	0	0

14. Protection of sources: granting and preserving confidentiality; disguising the nature of a source with a vested interest; otherwise withholding relevant information from the reader.

	Editors	
Response	1982	2005
Never	6	9
Less than once a year	8	9
About once or twice a year	16	20
Several times a year	35	30
About once a month	16	10
Two or three times a month	9	8
Nearly every week	7	4
Several times a week	4	10

15. Invasion of privacy: causing injury to feelings; disclosing embarrassing private facts.

	Editors	
Response	1982	2005
Never	5	8
Less than once a year	8	9
About once or twice a year	16	17
Several times a year	33	38
About once a month	18	6
Two or three times a month	12	8
Nearly every week	6	10
Several times a week	3	4

16. Economic temptations: accepting trips, meals, favors, loans, gifts, from sources or suppliers; heavy socializing with sources.

	Editors	
Response	1982	2005
Never	28	26
Less than once a year	10	17
About once or twice a year	31	23
Several times a year	18	24
About once a month	12	8

Two or three times a month	1	2
Nearly every week	1	0
Several times a week	1	0

17. Government secrecy: grand jury leaks; national security problems, including military secrets and diplomatic leaks.

Response	Editors	
	1982	2005
Never	15	20
Less than once a year	14	22
About once or twice a year	32	24
Several times a year	21	18
About once a month	12	2
Two or three times a month	2	7
Nearly every week	2	5
Several times a week	2	1

18. Civil disorder: publicizing rioters, terrorists, bomb threats, at the risk of encouraging imitators.

Response	Editors	
	1982	2005
Never	13	17
Less than once a year	26	25
About once or twice a year	32	29
Several times a year	24	27
About once a month	3	1
Two or three times a month	3	1
Nearly every week	1	0
Several times a week	0	0

19. Photos: violence; obscenity; hurt feelings.

Response	Editors	
	1982	2005
Never	9	3
Less than once a year	4	8
About once or twice a year	19	12
Several times a year	39	33
About once a month	14	19
Two or three times a month	5	11
Nearly every week	6	10
Several times a week	4	4

20. Pressure from advertisers: blurbs; business-office musts; pressure to keep things out of the paper or get them in.

	Editors	
Response	1982	2005
Never	21	27
Less than once a year	6	17
About once or twice a year	26	23
Several times a year	20	18
About once a month	11	6
Two or three times a month	6	6
Nearly every week	6	3
Several times a week	3	1

21. Fairness, balance and objectivity: allocating space to opposing interest groups or political candidates; providing right of reply to criticism.

	Editors	
Response	1982	2005
Never	2	3
Less than once a year	2	0
About once or twice a year	6	3
Several times a year	25	17
About once a month	15	8
Two or three times a month	13	18
Nearly every week	14	25
Several times a week	22	26

22. Conflict of interest: interest group activity by editors and publishers; service on boards and committees; campaign donations; stories involving financial interests of newspaper staff or management; spouse involvement.

	Editors	
Response	1982	2005
Never	17	14
Less than once a year	16	18
About once or twice a year	38	24
Several times a year	22	26
About once a month	4	8
Two or three times a month	2	7
Nearly every week	1	1
Several times a week	1	1

23. Use of reporters for non-news tasks: writing advertising supplements; gathering data for the company's financial decisions or labor relations objectives.

Response	Editors	
	1982	2005
Never	62	66
Less than once a year	15	20
About once or twice a year	15	7
Several times a year	7	5
About once a month	1	1
Two or three times a month	0	0
Nearly every week	1	1
Several times a week	0	0

24. Suppression of news to protect the community: factory relocations; school closings; highway expansion.

Response	Editors	
	1982	2005
Never	55	65
Less than once a year	12	17
About once or twice a year	18	8
Several times a year	5	8
About once a month	8	2
Two or three times a month	1	0
Nearly every week	2	0
Several times a week	0	0

25. Plagiarism: using material from other publications without attribution.

Response	Editors
	2005
Never	26
Less than once a year	25
About once or twice a year	25
Several times a year	21
About once a month	2
Two or three times a month	2
Nearly every week	0
Several times a week	0

26. Fabrication: writers making up quotes or creating fictitious events, people, or institutions.

Response	Editors 2005
Never	38
Less than once a year	32
About once or twice a year	16
Several times a year	12
About once a month	1
Two or three times a month	1
Nearly every week	0
Several times a week	0

Publisher & Editor Involvement

27. Newspapers vary greatly in the amount of involvement that publishers have in the news operations. Here are four statements describing different levels of publisher involvement. Regardless of how things work at your paper, which of the following statements comes closest to describing the way you think *publishers* ought to operate:

1. The publisher should always be involved in deciding what appears in his or her newspaper on a day-to-day basis.
2. The publisher should generally be involved in deciding what appears in his or her newspaper over the long run, but not on a daily basis.
3. The publisher should be involved in hiring good people to run the news operation, but not in deciding what appears in the paper. The publisher's only intervention in the news operation should be to hire or fire the editor.
4. The publisher should have nothing whatever to do with the news operation.

Response	Editors 1982	Editors 2005	Staff 1982	Staff 2005
Statement 1	2	2	1	4
Statement 2	58	48	54	29
Statement 3	36	48	43	59
Statement 4	5	2	2	8

28. Now that you have told us how publishers *should* operate, please indicate which of the four comes closest to the way things actually work at your paper.

1. The publisher is always involved in deciding what appears in the newspaper on a day-to-day basis.
2. The publisher is generally involved in deciding what appears in the newspaper over the long run, but not on a daily basis.
3. The publisher is involved in hiring good people to run the news operation, but not in deciding what appears in the paper. The publisher's only intervention in the news operation is to hire or fire the editor.
4. The publisher has nothing whatever to do with the news operation.

Response	Editors 1982	Editors 2005	Staff 1982	Staff 2005
Statement 1	3	4	9	8
Statement 2	61	50	53	50
Statement 3	32	42	29	39
Statement 4	4	4	9	4

29. One issue in some companies is how much editors should be involved in the company's marketing and financial plans. Which of the following statements best describes the role you think the *editor* should have at your company?

1. The editor should participate fully in financial planning and marketing decisions.
2. The editor should be kept fully informed in financial planning and marketing decisions, but should participate only when questions related to his specific expertise are involved.
3. The editor should be kept informed of financial planning and marketing decisions on a "need-to-know" basis, i.e., whenever his help is needed in carrying out the decisions.
4. The editor should be insulated from all financial planning and marketing decisions so that he can concentrate on putting out the paper.

Response	Editors 1982	Editors 2005	Staff 1982	Staff 2005
Statement 1	45	41	20	10
Statement 2	39	47	54	50
Statement 3	14	11	21	21
Statement 4	2	1	6	20

30. Which comes closest to describing the actual situation at your company?

1. The editor participates fully in financial planning and marketing decisions.
2. The editor is kept fully informed in financial planning and marketing decisions.
3. The editor is kept informed of financial planning and marketing decisions on a "need-to-know" basis, i.e., whenever his help is needed in carrying out the decisions.
4. The editor is insulated from all financial planning and marketing decisions so that he can concentrate on putting out the paper.

Response	Editors 1982	Editors 2005	Staff 1982	Staff 2005
Statement 1	28	39	11	22
Statement 2	33	41	38	43
Statement 3	35	19	45	30
Statement 4	4	1	6	4

31. How often does the publisher of your paper ask for special handling of an article about a company or organization which has some economic clout over your newspaper?

Response	Editors 1982	Editors 2005	Staff 1982	Staff 2005
Never	54	58	32	52
Less than once a year	12	21	18	20
About once or twice a year	19	15	20	16
Several times a year	11	4	23	8
About once a month	1	1	3	2
Two or three times a month	1	0	3	1
Nearly every week	1	0	1	1
Every week	0	0	0	1

32. How often does the publisher ask for special handling of an article about an organization or individual with whom he has strong social ties?

Response	Editors		Staff	
	1982	2005	1982	2005
Never	48	57	31	55
Less than once a year	14	19	10	15
About once or twice a year	19	15	24	16
Several times a year	16	7	23	11
About once a month	1	1	5	1
Two or three times a month	2	1	4	1
Nearly every week	0	0	2	1
Every week	0	1	0	1

33. How often does the publisher ask the editor to send a reporter on a non-news mission for the company: to influence legislation, for example, or gather information on the competition?

Response	Editors		Staff	
	1982	2005	1982	2005
Never	81	92	82	93
Less than once a year	12	6	10	5
About once or twice a year	5	2	6	1
Several times a year	2	1	2	1
About once a month	0	0	0	0
Two or three times a month	0	0	0	0
Nearly every week		0		0
Every week		0		0

Values

34. Newspaper people have different ideas about respecting pledges of confidentiality. Which of the following statements comes closest to your view?

1. A pledge of confidentiality to a source should always be kept no matter what the circumstances, even if it means a long jail term for the reporter and heavy financial cost to the newspaper.
2. A pledge of confidentiality should always be taken seriously, but it can be violated in unusual circumstances, e.g., when it is learned the source lied to the reporter.
3. A pledge of confidentiality can be broken if the editor and the reporter agree that the harm done by keeping it is greater than the damage caused by breaking it.
4. Pledges of confidentiality are largely rhetorical devices and not intended to be taken seriously.

	Editors		Staff	
Response	1982	2005	1982	2005
Statement 1	20	28	40	33
Statement 2	71	67	51	59
Statement 3	9	5	9	7
Statement 4	0	0	0	0

35. Under which of the following circumstances should a newspaper publish material from leaked grand jury transcripts?

1. Whenever the material is newsworthy.
2. Whenever the importance of the material revealed outweighs the damage to the system from breaching its security.
3. Only if the material exposes flaws in the working of the grand jury system itself, e.g., it shows the prosecutor to be acting improperly.
4. Never.

	Editors		Staff	
Response	1982	2005	1982	2005
Statement 1	19	36	32	31
Statement 2	60	54	49	50
Statement 3	15	8	13	14
Statement 4	7	2	7	5

36. A prominent citizen is vacationing alone in Key West, and his hotel burns down. The wire service story lists him among those who escaped uninjured and identifies the hotel as a popular gathering place for affluent gays. The citizen says he'll commit suicide if you publish his name in the story. Should the editor:

1. Publish the story in full.
2. Publish the story, but without mentioning the gay angle.
3. Publish the story, but without mentioning the local citizen.
4. Kill the story.

	Editors		Staff	
Response	1982	2005	1982	2005
Statement 1	41	30	46	33
Statement 2	52	59	43	49
Statement 3	7	10	10	16
Statement 4	0	0	0	1

37. An investigative reporter uses a computer to analyze criminal court records and writes a prize-winning series. A major computer manufacturer then offers to pay him $1,000 to speak at a seminar for reporters which it is sponsoring at a university. Which of the following best describes your view?

1. The reporter should be allowed to make the speech and accept the $1,000 from the computer manufacturer.
2. The reporter should be allowed to make the speech, but accept the $1,000 only if the honorarium is paid through the university.
3. The reporter should be allowed to make the speech, but not to accept the honorarium.
4. The reporter should not be allowed to make the speech.

	Editors		Staff	
Response	1982	2005	1982	2005
Statement 1	24	11	38	12
Statement 2	18	10	16	13
Statement 3	51	65	41	60
Statement 4	8	14	5	15

38. An investigative reporter does a thorough and praiseworthy exposé of inequalities in tax assessment practices. In the course of investigating for the story, he looks at his own assessment records and finds that a value-enhancing addition to his property was never recorded, and as a result, his taxes are $600 less than they should be. He reports this fact in the first draft of his story, but, later, at the urging of his wife, takes it out. Should the editor:

1. Insist that he leave the information in, even though it will raise the reporter's taxes.
2. Talk to the wife and try to persuade her that the reporter's honesty at leaving it in will be rewarded, somehow.
3. Leave it to the reporter to decide, but appeal to his conscience.
4. Not interfere.

	Editors		Staff	
Response	**1982**	**2005**	**1982**	**2005**
Statement 1	74	79	58	55
Statement 2	4	1	2	5
Statement 3	17	13	29	27
Statement 4	5	7	11	13

39. Easter Sunday is approaching, and the editor plans the traditional page-one recognition of the holiday: A banner, "He is Risen." Then a new publisher, who happens to be an agnostic, points out that the latest religious census shows the community to be six percent non-Christian. Should the editor:

1. Keep the Easter banner.
2. Reduce the headline in deference to the non-Christians in the community.
3. Limit the paper's coverage to specific religious-oriented events scheduled for that day.
4. Avoid any mention of Easter.

	Editors		Staff	
Response	**1982**	**2005**	**1982**	**2005**
Statement 1	50	29	42	26
Statement 2	4	12	4	15
Statement 3	46	57	53	58
Statement 4	1	1	1	1

40. Some newspaper companies in Florida donated money to a campaign to defeat a statewide referendum which, if passed, would have legalized gambling. Which of the following statements comes closest to your view on this action?

1. A newspaper that takes an editorial stand on an issue has a right, and possibly even a duty, to back up its belief with its money.
2. The contributions are justified if the referendum would have a detrimental effect on the business climate in which the newspaper operates.
3. The contributions should not have been made because they might lead readers to question the objectivity of the papers' news coverage.
4. No political contributions should ever be made by newspapers. The news and editorial columns make us powerful enough already, and adding money only indicates inappropriate hunger for more power.

Response	Editors		Staff	
	1982	2005	1982	2005
Statement 1	11	6	6	3
Statement 2	2	11	4	8
Statement 3	31	29	34	31
Statement 4	56	54	57	59

41. Do you think it is a good idea or a bad idea for a newspaper editor to serve on the board of another local company?

Response	Editors		Staff	
	1982	2005	1982	2005
Good idea	3	3	3	3
Bad idea	92	95	88	83
No difference	6	3	9	14

42. (IF BAD IDEA TO Q. 41) What if the company is non-profit, like a hospital or a symphony orchestra? Would the editor's serving on such a board be a good idea or a bad idea?

Response	Editors		Staff	
	1982	2005	1982	2005
Good idea	10	16	13	15
Bad idea	78	80	74	74
No difference	12	4	12	12

43. (IF BAD IDEA TO Q. 41) What if it was the board of a charitable enterprise like United Way or a local foundation?

Response	Editors		Staff	
	1982	2005	1982	2005
Good idea	2	16	1	19
Bad idea	92	76	91	69
No difference	6	8	8	13

44. (IF BAD IDEA TO Q. 41) How about a church vestry or PTA board?

Response	Editors		Staff	
	1982	2005	1982	2005
Good idea	9	36	5	24
Bad idea	40	46	63	54
No difference	43	19	33	22

45. Do you agree or disagree? A state news council, modeled after the National News Council, would be a good idea.

Response	Editors		Staff	
	1982	2005	1982	2005
Agree	29	22	49	56
Disagree	71	78	51	44

46. We'd like to know how involved *you* are in civic affairs. How many local, voluntary organizations do you belong to? Include churches, civic clubs, charitable organizations, veterans groups, etc.

Response	Editors		Staff	
	1982	2005	1982	2005
Mean	2.32	1.79	1.25	1.16

47. Different newspapers have different rules for deciding what is acceptable in advertising copy. At your newspaper, how often does the publisher ask the editor's advice when a question of acceptability arises?

Response	Editors		Staff	
	1982	2005	1982	2005
Always	6	12	1	7
Most of the time	8	13	6	8
Some of the time	35	37	14	25
Almost never	51	38	79	60

48. How often, to the best of your knowledge, does your paper publish editorial matter controlled by the business office on behalf of advertisers in the news columns (commonly known as "blurbs" or
"business office musts")?

Response	Editors 1982	Editors 2005	Staff 1982	Staff 2005
Never	76	85	61	75
Less than once a year	3	5	9	9
About once or twice a year	5	4	6	5
Several times a year	9	3	12	5
About once a month	1	1	3	4
Two or three times a month	2	1	3	1
Nearly every week	2	1	3	1
Every week	0	1	3	1
Several times a week	1	0	1	0
Daily	0	0	0	0

49. As you know, some newspaper companies are privately owned,
and some are at least partly owned by investors who buy and sell
stock on public exchanges. Do you think that whether a company is
publicly or privately owned makes any difference in the way it serves
its local community?

Response	Editors 1982	Editors 2005	Staff 1982	Staff 2005
Yes	38	54	39	60
No	62	46	61	40

50. (IF YES TO Q. 49) How frequently would you say the pressures
of being publicly owned hinder a newspaper's ability to serve the
local community?

Response	Editors 1982	Editors 2005	Staff 1982	Staff 2005
Often	16	31	10	28
Sometimes	53	46	60	55
Rarely	19	11	26	14
Never	12	12	4	3

51. Some newspaper people believe that every newspaper should
have a written code of ethics or set of guidelines that its staff could
consult when problems come up. Others say that every situation is

different, and each ethical problem needs to be considered on its own merits. Which comes closest to your belief?

Response	Editors		Staff	
	1982	2005	1982	2005
Written code	63	75	63	75
Case by case	37	26	37	25

52. Does your newspaper have a written code of ethics or set of guidelines?

Response	Editors		Staff	
	1982	2005	1982	2005
Yes	51	77	35	76
No	49	23	65	24

53. Some editors believe that opinion pages should have more leeway when it comes to policing factual and interpretive error. Others say opinion pages should be held to the same standards of accuracy as news pages. Which is closest to your belief?

1. Opinion pages should have more leeway.
2. Opinion pages should have the same accuracy standards as news pages.

	Editors	Staff
	2005	2005
Statement 1	18	16
Statement 2	82	84

State of the Newsroom

54. How would you rate the morale in your newsroom during the past few months? On a scale of 1 to 10, with 10 being the happiest possible newsroom and 1 being the least happy, where would you put yours?

Least   **Most**

1 2 3 4 5 6 7 8 9 10

	Editors		Staff	
Response	**1982**	**2005**	**1982**	**2005**
1	1	0	5	2
2	1	1	4	3
3	1	5	10	19
4	3	2	12	11
5	7	10	25	18
6	20	18	14	14
7	27	34	19	20
8	35	24	8	10
9	5	7	2	3
10	0	0	1	1
Mean	6.91	6.72	5.31	5.36

55. Thinking about the past 12 months, has your newsroom had layoffs or reduction in force through attrition in that period?

	Editors	Staff
Response	**2005**	**2005**
Layoffs	6	11
Reduction in force	29	30
Both	2	8
Neither	63	52